At David C Cook, we equip the local church around
the corner and around the globe to make disciples.
Come see how we are working together—go to
www.davidccook.org. Thank you!

DAVID C COOK

transforming lives together

LETTERS TO THE CHURCH

FRANCIS CHAN

DAVID C COOK

transforming lives together

LETTERS TO THE CHURCH
Published by David C Cook
4050 Lee Vance Drive
Colorado Springs, CO 80918 U.S.A.

Integrity Music Limited, a Division of David C Cook
Eastbourne, East Sussex BN23 6NT, England

The graphic circle C logo is a registered trademark of David C Cook.

All Scripture quotations are taken from the ESV® Bible (The Holy Bible,
English Standard Version®), copyright © 2001 by Crossway, a publishing
ministry of Good News Publishers. Used by permission. All rights reserved.
The author has added italics to Scripture quotations for emphasis.

LCCN 2018942853
ISBN 978-0-8307-7658-0
eISBN 978-0-8307-7583-5

© 2018 Crazy Love Ministries

The Team: Wendi Lord, Amy Konyndyk,
Nick Lee, Rachael Stevenson, Susan Murdock
Cover Design: Jim Elliston

Printed in the United States of America
First Edition 2018

1 2 3 4 5 6 7 8 9 10

062818

CONTENTS

ACKNOWLEDGMENTS

There were many people who contributed to this book, who helped me wrestle through everything from theology to logic to grammar. It was definitely a group effort, like most things in my life now.

Thanks mostly to the elders of We Are Church, who prayed faithfully for me: Kevin Kim, Kevin Shedden, Justin Clark, Rob Zabala, Sean Brakey, and Pira Tritasavit. You have modeled intimacy with Christ, and that has helped me prioritize the most important thing in life.

Special thanks to the writing team: Mark Beuving, who helped me edit and formulate thoughts once again; Kevin, Karmia, and Jeanne for helping structure the book; Sean for taking the time to strengthen some of my thoughts; Liz for freeing up my life, even though you quit on me. Last but not least, thanks to Mercy Chan, who saved me at the end. Who would have thought that my weirdest child would end up being so helpful?

Thanks to all the pastors at We Are Church for faithfully shepherding and loving the people: Denys Maslov, Nate Connelly, Joe Pemberton, David Manison, Chaz Meyers, Paul Meyers, Brian Kusunoki, Aaron Robison, Peter Gordon, Marcus Hung, Jon Kurien, Angel Velarde, Marcus Bailey, David Schaeffer, Ryan Takasugi, Isaiah Pekary, Matt Shiraki, Al Cortes, Kevin Lin, Brandon Miller, Felipe Anguiano, and Kent McCormick.

Thanks to Jim Elliston, who had to design two different covers for me since I changed the title.

Thanks to the media and digital marketing volunteers, who gave up many hours to help with this project.

Thanks to David C Cook for being the most supportive publisher and partner one can dream of.

Thanks to Paul Chan for keeping everything running smoothly at the office so I could be freed up to write.

Thanks to my wonderful wife, Lisa, who never complained about my busyness over the past few months. And to Ellie, Zeke, Claire, and Silas for being great and patient kids while Dad was writing.

1

THE DEPARTURE

Imagine you find yourself stranded on a deserted island with nothing but a copy of the Bible. You have no experience with Christianity whatsoever, and all you know about the Church will come from your reading of the Bible. How would you imagine a church to function? Seriously. Close your eyes for two minutes and try to picture "Church" as you would know it.

Now think about your current church experience. Is it even close?

Can you live with that?

SOME BACKGROUND

Eight years have passed since I left Cornerstone Church in Simi Valley, California, yet people are still asking me the same question: Why?

Why did you leave a church that was doing great things? Why would you leave all those people you loved?

Why did you leave the country when you seemed to be gaining influence? Did your beliefs change? Do you still love the Church?

You built a megachurch, started a college, wrote bestselling books, had a huge podcast following, and then you suddenly walked away from it all and moved your family to Asia. It just doesn't make sense!

While I am anxious to share what God has been teaching me recently, it's probably helpful to share about how God led me in the past. I want to clear up any confusion and give some insight on why I am writing this book.

First let me say that my years in Simi Valley were so good. I am literally smiling as I type this. I spent over sixteen years as pastor of Cornerstone, so my mind is filled with both hilarious and meaningful memories. So many faces come to mind, deep friendships, spiritual moments, and periods of awe over the things God was doing. I believe I will be spending eternity with many people who fell in love with Jesus during those years. Nothing can ever take that away.

WHY I LEFT MY MEGACHURCH

In 1994, when I was twenty-six years old, I decided to plant a church. It wasn't something I planned on doing. After all, I had been married for less than a month. Lisa and I were having a rough time at our church. The elders and the lead pastor had been fighting, which eventually led to the pastor's removal. The members were also fighting as they were divided on who was more wrong: the elders or the pastor. Everyone was discouraged by all the division. Sundays were far from uplifting, and I couldn't see how any of this could be pleasing to God. It was at that time I told my new bride I had a crazy idea: What if we started a church out of our house?

Even if there were only a dozen people in our living room, wouldn't it be better than what we had been experiencing? Lisa agreed, and so began Cornerstone Church in Simi Valley.

I was determined to create something different from what I had experienced before. This was my chance to build exactly the kind of church I wanted to be part of. I basically had three goals in mind. First, I wanted all of us to sing directly to God. And I mean really sing. I'm not talking about going through the motions of singing out of routine or guilt. Have you ever been part of a group of people actually singing directly to God? Singing with reverence and emotion? Singing as though God is really listening to their voices? That is a powerful experience, and I wanted it to be central to our new church.

Can be fake too.

It's judgment

11

Second, I wanted all of us to really hear the Word of God. We weren't going to be those people who gather together to listen to some self-help nonsense, nor were we going to ignore half the Bible. I wanted us to dig deeply into Scripture—even the passages that contradicted our logic and desires. I wanted the presentation of God's truth to be powerful, and I wanted us to take it seriously. So I began to preach week after week, verse by verse through the Bible. We all set out to truly hear everything the Word of God was saying to us.

And finally, I wanted all of us to live holy lives. I had seen too many Christians packed into too many churches who seemed to have no interest in actually doing what the Bible said. I couldn't get past the tragic irony of this. These people would come back week after week to hear from a Book that demands that they "be doers of the word, and not hearers only" (James 1:22), but they never seemed to do anything. Not that I was perfect or expected anyone else to be, but I wanted our church to be a group of people who pushed one another toward action. It didn't make sense to teach the Scriptures without expecting change. So from the very beginning, we challenged one another to action.

And that was basically it. If we could move toward these three goals, I would be happy.

I wish you could have seen how God worked in those early days! Things took off! Nothing was perfect, but there was so much excitement. Visitors found our services compelling, so we kept growing. We rented the local middle-school cafeteria.

Eventually we moved into a converted former liquor store right next to Chuck E. Cheese's. After outgrowing that, we finally bought our own building. Before long, even that building had to undergo a major expansion. God was stirring hearts, the number of people who were gathering to sing and hear the Word of God kept growing, and we had to keep adding services. We were up to two Saturday night services and three Sunday morning services when we realized we needed to plant campuses in neighboring towns. It was unreal. Our podcast was gaining subscribers every day from all over the world, we were pouring out our hearts to God with our singing, and there was great conviction.

There was so much life at our services. People would cheer as I would talk about the ways their money helped needy people in Third-World countries. Many couples began adopting children out of the foster care system. Our attendance and offering climbed consistently for years. Baptisms happened every weekend. Lives were being changed. There was no church I would rather have been a part of. But over the years, I couldn't shake the feeling that something was still missing. It wasn't a problem with the church members or with the staff God brought to help me lead. We were successful in staying on target with the goals that had set the DNA of the church. But something was off.

There came a point when some of the elders of the church began to question whether our idea of success was somehow inadequate. Was this really what the Church is meant to be? Is this all God had in mind when He created His Church in the first place? We began to wonder whether our definition of a church actually fit God's definition. The elders of Cornerstone sought the Scriptures with me and challenged my thinking as to what Jesus wanted of the Church. These men of God encouraged and spurred me on through this season, and it was a joy to serve alongside them.

One of the main things that we questioned was the level of love we had for one another. Cornerstone was by most standards a pretty loving church. But next to the example of the early church in the New Testament, it just fell flat. Jesus said the world should know us by our love (John 13:35). As elders, we came to the painful conclusion that when unbelievers came to our services, they weren't observing anything supernatural about the way we loved one another.

Another issue we saw was how everything had grown to be very dependent on one person. Even as we talked about building a new facility and the expenses involved with that, the elders questioned what would happen if I was no longer the pastor. Would Cornerstone become like so many other churches, stuck with a giant empty building? Again, this is a big issue! Not just because of the waste of money but because no church should be that dependent on one person. We wanted people to come to Cornerstone to experience almighty God and the moving of the Holy Spirit—not to hear Francis Chan.

Because my leadership was so prominent in the church, I also began to see that it was holding back others who should have been leading. As I started to encourage some of my staff members and elders to leave and began releasing them into new ministries, I saw how much they grew from being given the opportunity to pastor.

The Bible tells us that every member of the body has a gift necessary to the functioning of the Church. When I looked at what went on in Cornerstone, I saw a few other people and me using our gifts, while thousands just came and sat in the sanctuary for an hour and a half and then went home. The way we had structured the church was stunting people's growth, and the whole body was weaker for it.

It was humbling to discuss biblical commands we had neglected. We decided we wanted to bring change into the church. At the time, I didn't realize how difficult it was going to be. I became frustrated with the way things were, but I didn't have clarity on what we needed to become. I was certain that things needed to change, but I didn't know how to make it happen. Some of my messages probably sounded like the rants of an angry old man rather than a wise and loving shepherd guiding his sheep to greener pastures.

We tried a lot of different things. We tried having me preach less to release some of the associate pastors into holding greater responsibility, but we found that it became hard for them to lead while still in my shadow, so to speak. We tried getting people to plant smaller churches out of their homes, but people had grown accustomed to the benefits of childcare and preaching at the big service. Eventually they would give up. There was even a time when I stepped away from the main gathering in Simi Valley and helped launch several home gatherings in LA County. It started to gain traction, but then I was needed back in Simi. It was a difficult time. I give the church credit for enduring all the trial and error going on. Eventually people started to get tired and frustrated, and a small exodus began.

CHANGING THE RULES

One young person in the church articulated it so well. He said it felt as if the rules were suddenly changed on him. He explained that for years he was taught salvation was a free gift and the gospel meant he could have a personal relationship with Jesus. It would be like someone gifting him a pair of ice skates. In excitement, he went to the skating rink and learned to do all sorts of tricks. He enjoyed this and did it for years. Now suddenly he was being told that the skates were actually given to him because he was supposed to be a part of our hockey team working together to pursue a championship. He wasn't supposed to just twirl around by himself. That's a huge difference! While he did not disagree biblically, it would take time to realign his thinking and lifestyle.

As I look back now, I realize that I didn't lead very well. I was anxious for change, but I didn't have a good plan, and I wasn't patiently helping the people get their minds around such a major paradigm shift. I ended up frustrating some of the people I loved. When I left Cornerstone, it was with the genuine belief that my time was done and the church could move forward better without me.

There were lots of other factors as well. When people ask why I left, it's really hard to point to just one thing. I was losing peace and humility as my popularity as a speaker and author grew.

Social media had just been invented, so now I had total strangers praising or cursing me. I didn't know how to handle so much criticism and flattery. I wanted to run from it all. I also struggled with the sheer number of Bible-teaching churches in our city when I knew there were many places on earth without a strong Christian witness. It didn't seem like it would require much faith to just keep doing what I was doing, and I wanted to live by faith. I was also very unclear as to how to lead Cornerstone into the future. Needless to say, it was a very confusing time.

Leaving Cornerstone was definitely not an easy decision. During the season when I was still wrestling with whether that would be the best thing to do, I went to preach at an event. Lisa came with me, and on the way there we had a conversation that shocked me. My debate about staying in Simi Valley up to this point had been completely internal. We had never talked about leaving before. Cornerstone was our baby, and Simi Valley was our home. But when I finally decided to ask her what she saw us doing for the rest of our lives, she surprised me by saying she felt as if we had done all we could do in Simi Valley and it was time to move on. She even brought up going to another country, which was exactly what I had been considering.

Fifteen minutes later, I got a phone call from my friend Jeff, who was a member of Cornerstone. He told me he felt like God wanted him to tell me something: "Just go. Don't worry about the church. There are others here who will step up and take care of the church." That was so crazy to me! There was no way he could have known the conversation Lisa and I just had. No one knew what was going on in my mind.

After that, things kept falling into place, and I felt greater and greater peace about leaving. It got to the point where Lisa and I felt as if we would be disobedient if we didn't leave. We ended up selling our house in Simi Valley and taking our family of six at the time overseas to India, Thailand, and China. It was an amazing adventure that knit our family so close together and helped us refocus on the mission. I saw such fearless dedication and boldness from the pastors in India, who had renounced everything for the Lord. We witnessed the simplicity of the lifestyles in rural Thailand and the joy of the men and women who faithfully served widows and orphans day in and day out. In China I saw the gospel spreading like wildfire as people endured and even rejoiced in persecution.

Throughout this whole time, Lisa and I were praying with the family about where God would have us live. We almost ended up staying in Hong Kong. We were looking at housing options as well as schools for the kids. Then one day I really felt as if the Lord was speaking to me.

Please understand I do not say that lightly. My background is one that is extremely conservative. I trust only what I see written in the Bible. While my theology left some room for hearing directly from God, I'm not sure I had ever heard it before that day. Again, I'm not sure I heard from the Lord, but I had more peace in obeying what I thought I heard than in ignoring it. I really believe He was telling me to go back to the States and plant churches. While overseas, I had gotten to see a glimpse of what the church could be and the power it could have, and I felt like God wanted me to take that vision back. I was pretty scared of what I thought God was communicating to me. It felt like He was asking me to do something I did not have the intelligence or leadership skills to accomplish.

It was a sad day when I told Lisa and the kids that I felt God wanted me back in the States. We were so happy overseas. We were closer as a family, more dependent on God, and more fixated on eternal matters. While there were feelings of fear when we left the United States, now there was greater fear in returning. We didn't want to lose our focus.

THE JOURNEY HOME

I'll spare you some details, but we eventually ended up in San Francisco mainly because my brother had a one-bedroom apartment we could stay in. I didn't have much of a plan. I just wanted to live as biblically as I knew how. In my prayers, I told the Lord I wanted to live like Christ, and it seemed like Jesus knew exactly whom to call as His disciples. I asked for that same grace: that I would be able to just walk around the city sharing the gospel, eventually meeting the people He would call me to disciple.

I made some friends over the first year, and we started a ministry where we ministered to the poor in the Tenderloin district of San Francisco. We fed the homeless and went door to door to pray for people in low-income housing. It was scary at times, but I loved the fact that I was living by faith in America. I was put in many uncomfortable situations, but it felt right. We saw God answer prayers in so many powerful ways, even though it didn't result in many true conversions.

I remember asking my kids what they felt after one of our first outreaches. Rachel, my oldest daughter, blurted out, "It felt like we jumped out of the Bible." I knew exactly what she meant. We were experiencing something in America that was congruent with what we read about in the New Testament! We felt alive, on an adventure that required faith, and it was right here in our backyard.

While the daily outreaches were going well and we enjoyed living by faith, we hadn't yet planted a church. I saw weaknesses in our ministry because it wasn't grounded in a strong, elder-led church. Knowing this was my calling, we gathered some of our new friends into our home and started a church. Twenty years after launching Cornerstone out of a living room, here we were again. My wonderful wife and a group of friends, sitting in a living room, asking God to build His Church through us.

It has been five years now since we started We Are Church, and things are so different this time around. Lisa and I have grown in our understanding of Scripture and God's design for the Church. God has graciously shown me the good fruit from my Cornerstone days as well as some of the fundamental mistakes I made early on. Hopefully, I can help others avoid some traps I fell into.

I am writing this during one of the happiest and most peaceful seasons of my life. It's not because life is easy. It's not. The peace has come from knowing God more deeply than ever. While I believe I have loved Jesus for years, it feels totally different now. Lately I have become obsessed with knowing and experiencing Him. The strangest part about this season of my life is that my intimacy with God has been directly tied to my connection with the Church. This is really weird for me because for years, I felt closest to God when I was away from people and alone in my prayer room. For the first time in my life, I actually feel closer to God while praying alongside my church family! It's as if I can sense His actual presence in the room with us. It makes me want to stay in a room with them all because I want to get as close to Jesus as possible. Just the other day, a one-hour teaching session spontaneously turned into thirteen hours of prayer! We were enjoying His presence together so much that no one wanted to leave!

One day the Lord may call me somewhere else on this earth, but right now I selfishly hope He doesn't. I don't want to be separated from this family. I love them because they bring me closer to Jesus. I have never felt less alone or more secure.

BIG PROBLEMS

I'm often sad when I speak to Christians across the United States because I don't hear many people speaking this way. Instead, I hear people complaining about their churches. I have spoken to many who have left altogether. This is a serious problem! I hope you haven't just grown calloused to it. This should break our hearts every time. The Church has real issues, but Jesus still refers to the Church as His body, His Bride! We must love His Bride, not gripe about her or leave her.

It is true that some who have abandoned the Church are rebellious and arrogant, but I believe there are others who are just confused. They love Jesus but have a hard time finding the connection between what they read in Scripture and what they experience in the Church. I'm not condoning their actions. After all, it is commanded by God that we gather with other believers and stir them to action (Heb. 10:24–25). I am saying only that some of their concerns have biblical grounding and should be addressed. Even in writing this book, I hope to encourage the wanderers to return. The Scriptures tell me you are indispensable and the body cannot function perfectly without you.

This is definitely the most difficult book I have written, mainly because I have been trying to stay mindful of 1 Thessalonians 5:14. Here God tells us that we should rebuke those who are rebellious and encourage those who are faint-hearted. That's doable if you know your people well enough to determine what they need. The problem with a book to the masses is that some of you need a hug and will feel kicked and some of you need to be kicked but will feel encouraged! To the lovers of Jesus who are feeling discouraged, I pray this book gives you hope for what is possible. To those who knowingly or subconsciously are harming the Church, I pray God gives you the grace to repent. It recently dawned on me that Jesus wrote seven different letters to seven different churches in Revelation 2 and 3. I'm trying to write to thousands of different churches with just one book! And Jesus writes better than me.

After I finished writing this book, I found that it read less like a book and more like a collection of connected but independent letters. Each chapter/letter addresses a different issue your church may or may not need to work on. I prayed that the Holy Spirit would help you discern which letters you and your church must take to heart. This book is not about obscure details I found in Leviticus but rather about the most obvious commands repeated throughout the entire Bible. I've tried to pay attention to the times when God seems most bothered by what His people were doing. Many want to change the Church, but it is often motivated by personal preference rather than biblical conviction. I am trying to point out only the most obvious biblical truths about God's desire for His Bride—truths that none of us can afford to ignore.

There are times when God hates our worship. There are churches He wants shut down. So often we assume that as long as we show up to worship, God is pleased. The Bible tells a different story (Amos 5:21–24; Isa. 58:1–5; Mal. 1:6–14; 1 Cor. 11:17–30; Rev. 2:5; 3:15–16).

Since the beginning of time, there has been worship God loves and worship He rejects. As I examine the state of the Christian Church today, I can't help but think that God is displeased with many of the churches in America.

I don't say that lightly. And I say it not because of what I feel but because of what I read in Scripture. My hope is that you read this book with a Bible at your side to check whether I am twisting the Scriptures or just stating the obvious. This isn't meant to be an attack or a debate. I'd like to think we are on the same team, all seeking to pursue the kind of Church that pleases Him most.

A HUMBLE WARNING

Nowadays people are eager to fight. Many are on edge, waiting for anyone to misspeak so they can pounce. It is in this environment that the Lord tells us to be eager to maintain unity (Eph. 4:3). I am trying to write with a spirit of unity. While some of the things I write may sound critical, I really am trying to speak in a spirit of grace and unity. One of the worst things that could happen is for angry people to take these words and proudly confront their church leadership. There is enough division and arrogance in the Church already. I believe there is a way to show kindness and grace toward one another without abandoning our convictions.

For those who are not in church leadership, be mindful that this is a very difficult time to lead. I have been in leadership positions for over thirty years. There has never been a time like this.

Social media gives everyone a voice, so everyone chooses to raise theirs. Voices are plentiful; followers are not. Strong opinions are applauded; humility is not. I am not saying that changes do not need to be made among leaders; I am simply calling for grace. Imagine how difficult it would be to coach a team where each player refuses to follow because he or she has a better plan than the coach. Welcome to the American Church in the twenty-first century. Let's exercise some humility.

We see such a refreshing mind-set in young David. Do you remember the times when David refused to harm Saul? In 1 Samuel 24 and 26, David had already been anointed as the rightful king of Israel, and King Saul by this point was a murderous, power-hungry lunatic. David had two perfect opportunities to remove Saul from power and claim the throne he had been promised, yet he refused to take matters into his own hands: "The LORD forbid that I should do this thing to my lord, the LORD's anointed, to put out my hand against him, seeing he is the LORD's anointed" (24:6).

Why does this attitude seem so foreign? Saul was a terrible leader who had actively turned against God, but David somehow had a holy fear of harming those God had placed in authority. Nowadays, if a leader makes a mistake, no matter how small or innocent, we are quick to criticize and move on. Forgiveness is rare and almost nonexistent toward ministers. We flippantly use the strongest language to rant against leadership. I'm not arguing in favor of abusive leaders, nor am I saying that every leader has God's blessing. All I'm asking is that we show some humility and respect, even to those who don't deserve it. Let's be people of grace.

JUST OPEN THE DOOR

God designed the Church to be much more than what the majority of us experience in America. There are many of us who believe this and want change. The good news is that God wants this change even more than we do. And He doesn't just want these changes; He commands them! We can move forward in confidence, knowing God wouldn't command us to do something unless He also empowered us for the task.

> *"Those whom I love, I reprove and discipline, so be zealous and repent. Behold, I stand at the door and knock. If anyone hears my voice and opens the door, I will come in to him and eat with him, and he with me. The one who conquers, I will grant him to sit with me on my throne, as I also conquered and sat down with my Father on his throne."*
> Revelation 3:19–21

After giving a very strong rebuke to the church of Laodicea for being lukewarm, Jesus simply asked them to open the door. Before you get overwhelmed by all that is wrong with the Church, remember that He is not placing an insurmountable burden on your shoulders. He is asking you to fellowship with Him and join Him in what He is doing. We should be filled with faith and anticipation, remembering what He did at the Red Sea and the empty tomb. Take a deep breath. Lay all your stress at His feet. Explain to Him your confusion regarding the difference you see between your church and the Church you read about. Tell Him your dissatisfaction with the lack of power in your life.

THE CLOCK IS TICKING

"Look carefully then how you walk, not as unwise
but as wise, making the best use of the time, because
the days are evil. Therefore do not be foolish, but
understand what the will of the Lord is."

Ephesians 5:15–17

I became a grandpa recently. It's weird to be able to type that sentence. The older I get, the more aware I am that the end is near. There is no time to care about what I want in the Church. There's no time to worry about what others are looking for in a church. I will be facing Him soon, so I have to stay focused on His desires. Typically when I speak at a conference, there is a countdown clock letting me know how much time I have remaining on the stage. Sometimes I pretend that the clock is a countdown of my life. I imagine that I'll be standing face-to-face with God when that timer expires. This gives me courage to say everything I think He would want me to say. If I really was going to die, I would care very little about people's complaints. I would be obsessed with seeing the face of God and wanting His approval.

I have the same thought now. If I knew I was going to die right after writing this book, what would I write? If I didn't worry about the fallout but sought only to be faithful to God, how would this book read? I have tried to write from this perspective.

2

SACRED

I was bothered the first time I read about God killing Uzzah just because he tried to keep the ark of the covenant from falling. Uzzah touched the ark because the cart it was riding on hit a pothole (2 Sam. 6). It seemed like a trivial mistake with good intentions. Sure, God had forbidden anyone from touching the ark, but what was Uzzah supposed to do? Let the holy ark of God fall to the ground?

Isn't it a little puzzling that King Saul's sacrifice cost him the kingdom (1 Sam. 13)? After all, he waited seven days for Samuel the priest to come and make the offering, but he didn't show up when he said he would. To me, it seems noble that Saul offered the sacrifice because he didn't want to go to war without first acknowledging God. Now the kingdom would be torn from him?

Or what about Moses, who didn't get to see the Promised Land because he struck the rock rather than speaking to it (Num. 20)? After everything Moses went through, was it such a big crime to be frustrated with the people and strike the rock in anger?

Then there are Ananias and Sapphira. They were both struck dead because they lied about how much money they donated to the church (Acts 5). And this is in the New Testament! Really, who hasn't exaggerated?

To top it off, Paul told the Corinthians that many of them were sick and some had even died because they celebrated Communion in an unworthy manner (1 Cor. 11:30). If Paul wasn't exaggerating, could we be one sip away from death?

To us, many situations in Scripture involve a punishment that was too severe for the crime. But why do we feel this way?

We don't understand what it means for something to be "sacred." We live in a human-centered world among people who see themselves as the highest authority. We are quick to say things like "That isn't fair!" because we believe we deserve certain rights as humans. Yet we give little thought to the rights God deserves as God. Even in the Church we can act as though God's actions should revolve around us. The stories in Scripture are meant to show us that there exists something of greater value than our existence and rights. There are things that belong to God. Sacred things. His ark of the covenant, His command to Moses, His offerings in the temple, His Holy Spirit, His Holy Communion, His sacred Church. In all the above situations, people rushed into something sacred and paid the price. We shouldn't be surprised; we should be humbled. We have all done things more irreverent than those mentioned above. Let's thank God for His mercy and tread more carefully into sacred matters.

RUSHING INTO THE SACRED

We live in a world where people carelessly rush into things. If we don't rush, we will be passed up and miss out. So we frantically follow the pattern of the world and ignore the fact that God calls us to act differently. Productivity is no sin, but when it comes to the sacred, God commands us to proceed with caution. Others may treat these things as common, but we cannot. While others quickly judge God's actions and question His commands, we are to be careful even to speak His name. We don't carelessly question His actions or inaction. Instead, we pray, "Hallowed be your name" (Matt. 6:9; Luke 11:2). While others rush into prayer with opinions and demands, we cautiously approach His throne in reverence. Like the high priest entering the Holy of Holies, we are to treat prayer as sacred.

> *"Guard your steps when you go to the house of God. To draw near to listen is better than to offer the sacrifice of fools, for they do not know that they are doing evil. Be not rash with your mouth, nor let your heart be hasty to utter a word before God, for God is in heaven and you are on earth. Therefore let your words be few. For a dream comes with much business, and a fool's voice with many words."*
>
> Ecclesiastes 5:1–3

I don't know whether you've noticed, but young people are speaking more quickly and even abbreviating words so they can squeeze the greatest number of words into a ten-second slot. The world speaks quickly and loudly. It is tempting to speak faster and scream louder so your voice will not be drowned out. But we must avoid that temptation. The Bible is clear: those who talk a lot sin a lot. We can never believe that we must sin in order to have greater impact.

> *"Know this, my beloved brothers: let every person be quick to hear, slow to speak, slow to anger."*
>
> James 1:19

> *"When words are many, transgression is not lacking, but whoever restrains his lips is prudent."*
>
> Proverbs 10:19

I have struggled in writing this book because I am addressing such a sacred topic. I have not always treated the Church as sacred. I spent years doing "whatever works" to get people's attention. I have joined millions of Americans in being too quick to speak and too sure about my opinions. Over the last few years, I have spent time crying in the presence of God, confessing my arrogance.

Part of me wants to stop speaking about the sacred things of God. There were many times when I wanted to stop writing this book, and I seriously thought about deleting it rather than publishing it. Being silent felt safer. Not only could I save myself from all the criticism I will receive, but I could protect myself from wrongly speaking about God. But that train of thought assumes it is never sinful to stay silent. I'm not trying to equate myself with an Old Testament prophet, but when I think about the things God has laid on my heart, I resonate with Jeremiah's dilemma. God gave him hard things to say to His people, and Jeremiah wanted to stop speaking. But he couldn't.

> *"For the word of the LORD has become for me a reproach*
> *and derision all day long. If I say, 'I will not mention*
> *him, or speak any more in his name,' there is in my*
> *heart as it were a burning fire shut up in my bones,*
> *and I am weary with holding it in, and I cannot."*
>
> Jeremiah 20:8–9

So I am proceeding with reverent caution. To treat God's Church as sacred demands careful and humble teaching. Here is my best attempt.

SACRED MYSTERY

There is no greater honor on earth than to be part of God's Church.

When was the last time you were awestruck by the fact that you are part of Christ's body? Have you ever marveled at this privilege?

> *"For no one ever hated his own flesh,*
> *but nourishes and cherishes it, just*
> *as Christ does the church, because*
> *we are members of his body."*
> Ephesians 5:29–30

Every believer needs to stare at those verses long enough to be stunned. I mean really stunned. Paul referred to it as a profound mystery. If achievement is your idol, you won't make time for mystery. You will rush to the next sentence so you can finish this book rather than meditate on the miracle that you are a human being who is currently joined to a God "who dwells in unapproachable light" (1 Tim. 6:16).

"This mystery is profound, and I am saying
that it refers to Christ and the church."

Ephesians 5:32

Slow down long enough to marvel.

The sun is ninety-three million miles away, and you are unable to stare at it.[1] You obviously can't touch the sun and live, so how is it possible that we are currently attached to the One who shines brighter than the sun? High angels cover themselves with their wings in His presence (Isa. 6:2), yet you are a member of His body. Why would Someone so extraordinary choose to care for you like His own arm?

Please tell me you didn't just keep reading. Please tell me you paused for even a minute to worship. You can't be that busy. It's no wonder we aren't known as those who "rejoice with joy that is inexpressible" (1 Pet. 1:8). We don't make time to meditate on His mysteries.

A SMALL PIECE OF THE TEMPLE

One of my favorite scenes in Scripture is the dedication of the temple in 2 Chronicles 7. I wish I could have been there to see it. Imagine being alive at that moment.

"As soon as Solomon finished his prayer, fire came down
from heaven and consumed the burnt offering and the

sacrifices, and the glory of the LORD filled the temple.
And the priests could not enter the house of the LORD,
because the glory of the LORD filled the LORD's house.
When all the people of Israel saw the fire come down
and the glory of the LORD on the temple, they bowed
down with their faces to the ground on the pavement
and worshiped and gave thanks to the LORD, saying,
'For he is good, for his steadfast love endures forever.'"

2 Chronicles 7:1–4

Can you imagine watching fire come down from heaven? What is God's glory like? I imagine my heart pounding. I picture myself struggling to even breathe and keep from fainting. Then there's the thrill of worshipping with other believers in the middle of it all! The temple was the place where heaven intersected with earth. A glimpse of His glory was made visible to human eyes.

The New Testament describes something even greater. The fact that I covet the Old Testament experience is an indication that I don't appreciate the new reality as I should.

"So then you are no longer strangers and aliens, but you
are fellow citizens with the saints and members of the
household of God, built on the foundation of the apostles
and prophets, Christ Jesus himself being the cornerstone,
in whom the whole structure, being joined together, grows

into a holy temple in the Lord. In him you also are being
built together into a dwelling place for God by the Spirit."

Ephesians 2:19–22

I would give anything to stand outside the temple and watch God's glory descend. But I get something so much better: I am literally a part of the temple itself! Somehow by the blood of Jesus, I became worthy of joining with others to form a dwelling place for God! Peter described us as "living stones" (1 Pet. 2:5). You are a stone in the same structure in which the apostles and prophets are the foundation and Jesus Himself is the cornerstone (Eph. 2:20)! When Paul talked about this concept, he used the plural form of *you* and the singular form of *temple*. We are all joined together to form one house for God. Somehow I am a block of a temple that transcends time and space. And because the structure is a temple, this means that God makes His home among us! You should be bursting out of your skin at this point!

Don't try to solve the mystery; just stare at it.

When Paul explained the mystery to the Corinthians, he added a terrifying warning.

"Do you not know that you are God's temple and
that God's Spirit dwells in you? If anyone destroys
God's temple, God will destroy him. For God's
temple is holy, and you are that temple."

1 Corinthians 3:16–17

Think back to the scene in 2 Chronicles 7. When the fire came down and God's glory filled the temple, would you have considered taking a sledgehammer and striking the temple? Of course not! Then why are we so quick to gossip, slander leadership, and divide the Church?

If anyone destroys God's temple, God will destroy that person.

Why is God so harsh about this? Paul explained that God's temple is sacred, and we—collectively—are that temple. Every time you speak evil about a member of the Church, it is like taking a sledgehammer to the temple. Are you sure you want to keep doing that?

Let's be careful with our words and actions. We are dealing with something sacred. Let's stay on the right side of His protection. Maybe this is why Paul said in Titus 3:10, "As for a person who stirs up division, after warning him once and then twice, have nothing more to do with him." We can't be enablers of division. God hates this sin too much. His temple is too sacred.

We live in a culture today where we are used to evaluating and giving our opinion on everything. Whether it's the pizza we ate, our Uber driver, the movie we saw, or our friend's picture on social media, everything is set up for us to be able to critique and compare. So in the Church, rather than marveling at the incredible mystery that we are a part of God's body, we critique the leadership, the music, the programs, and anything else we can think of. We point out the flaws in our pastor's sermon with the same conviction we critique a movie star's acting or our favorite team's recent loss. Could it be that we are taking a sledgehammer to the temple in so doing?

Remember that the temple was the location where God chose to live on earth. And now the Church is that temple. We are that temple. Consider this: 2 Chronicles 7—when the temple was dedicated—was not the only time fire fell from heaven onto the temple. It also happened in Acts 2 when the Church was born. The disciples were united and praying when tongues of fire fell on them. They were the temple. Fire fell on them. And you know the rest of the story.

A SMALL PIECE OF HEAVEN

You are a part of something much bigger than yourself, something sacred. Through Jesus' sacrifice you have been joined to His Church. Because of this, you are not only a part of God's sacred temple but also apart of the heavenly community. This is huge!

Take some time to read Revelation 4–5 as it describes the scene in heaven. This section begins with a majestic picture of God on His throne. The scene is busy and intense: the four living creatures are declaring His holiness, the seven spirits of God are blazing, myriads of angels are praising Jesus with loud voices, and the twenty-four elders are flat on their faces while laying their crowns before Him. Then in 5:8, we finally appear.

> *"And when he had taken the scroll, the four living*
> *creatures and the twenty-four elders fell down before*
> *the Lamb, each holding a harp, and golden bowls*
> *full of incense, which are the prayers of the saints."*
>
> Revelation 5:8

There you are! Did you see it? Those are your prayers in the bowl of incense! Isn't that awesome? We get to be part of this unbelievable scene!

Maybe you feel a bit insulted by this. You're thinking, *That's it? My only part is that my prayers are lumped in with the prayers of all other believers to form a bowl of incense?* Don't worry—you're also mentioned in verse 13 when your voice joins the chorus of billions.

> *"And I heard every creature in heaven and on*
> *earth and under the earth and in the sea, and all*
> *that is in them, saying, 'To him who sits on the*
> *throne and to the Lamb be blessing and honor*
> *and glory and might forever and ever!'"*
>
> Revelation 5:13

What is a tremendous, unspeakable honor may feel insufficient for those who are used to being god of their own blogs and Twitter accounts. It feels insignificant to those who have erected their own shrines on Facebook and Instagram, filled with beautiful pictures of themselves.

Herein lies the danger of clamoring for attention: we don't realize that true joy comes from the opposite. Joy comes as we stand among those Jesus has redeemed and get lost in a sea of worship, becoming fully a part of something sacred.

Gathering with the Church should lead us to holy ground. You get to come and worship Someone else, with someone else. You get to pour out love to Him by serving those around you and considering them more important than yourself. It's not about you. And you are glad it's not about you. Because this is something far greater than you. It is sacred.

A SMALL PART OF AN ETERNAL PLAN

Have you ever stopped to think about the fact that you are part of an eternal plan? Seriously think about this. Your existence didn't begin at conception. You began in the mind of God before the foundation of this earth. Meditate on this. Few things will make you feel smaller ... or bigger.

"Even as he chose us in him before the foundation of the world, that we should be holy and blameless before him. In love he predestined us for adoption to himself as sons through Jesus Christ, according to the purpose of his will."

Ephesians 1:4–5

Far from being an accident, you and I are part of a brilliant plan that started before planet Earth and continues beyond it. This is why self-deprecation is as wicked as slandering God's Church. We are belittling the creation of something God has planned and crafted. He chose us before the foundation of the world, knew us before He made us (Jer. 1:5), and drew up works for us before we were even created (Eph. 2:10). He had plans for His sacred Church and included us in those plans. This thought should bring tremendous peace to our often-stressed souls. The more I think about it, the more honored I feel to be chosen as part of God's eternal plan for the Church.

If you're not fascinated by your inclusion in His Church yet, it may help you to know that there are beings in heaven that stare at the Church in wonder.

"To me, though I am the very least of all the saints, this grace was given, to preach to the Gentiles the unsearchable riches of Christ, and to bring to light for everyone what is the plan of the mystery hidden for ages in God, who created all things, so that through the church the

manifold wisdom of God might now be made known
to the rulers and authorities in the heavenly places."
Ephesians 3:8–10

Think about what this is saying. God wanted to show the heavenly beings His incomparable wisdom … so He created the Church! I believe we have a sacred responsibility to function as His Church in such a way that the rulers in heavenly places can marvel at God's wisdom. They ought to see a oneness in us that displays God's brilliant plan.

Two verses earlier, Paul explained that the great mystery God is now revealing is Gentiles becoming members of the same body as the Jews because of what Jesus did on the cross. This is the divine mystery that was hidden in God for ages! The grand reveal that heavenly authorities were anticipating has arrived. The curtain is drawn back, and they gasp as they see … the Church. No way! This is unreal! Through the cross, people of every nation and tongue become members of one body? Amazing! God Himself is joining His creation and allowing them to be a part of His body? Unbelievable! This was His plan all along. There was going to come a day when almighty God would dwell with people of all races. They would be brought to complete unity, forming one temple, which would be a dwelling place for God!

Do you see why all this matters so much? Many today treat the Church as optional, as some outdated way to connect to

God that has long outlived its usefulness. They'd rather connect with God on their own, in their own way, without all the weird people making things more difficult. We can empathize with many of their feelings about the Church. But when we see the Church from God's perspective, when we appreciate it according to God's design, we're left in wonder. Who but God could come up with such a beautiful and ingenious plan?

I can't help but see our own lameness in failing to see the beauty in God's design for the Church. Heavenly beings are shocked by God's Church, while many on earth yawn. The early church didn't need the energetic music, great videos, attractive leaders, or elaborate lighting to be excited about being a part of God's body. The pure gospel was enough to put them in a place of awe.

Aren't you at least a little embarrassed that you have needed the extra stuff? It's not all your fault. For decades church leaders like myself have lost sight of the powerful mystery inherent in the Church and have instead run to other methods to keep people interested. In all honesty, we have trained you to become addicted to lesser things. We have cheapened something sacred, and we must repent.

3

THE ORDER

Imagine you walked into a restaurant and ordered a steak. Twenty minutes later, the waiter comes back and puts a plate of spaghetti in front of you, claiming it's the best spaghetti you'll ever try. Would you be happy about it? No, you would send it back because it wasn't what you ordered. It wasn't even close!

I feel like this is what we have done with the Church. God gave us His "order" for the Church. He told us precisely what He wanted through His commandments in the Bible. In our arrogance, we created something we think works better. Rather than diligently studying His commands and delivering exactly what

He asked for, we have been influenced by so many other things. We think about what we want, what others would want, what others are doing. In the spirit of Cain, we bring an offering we think He should accept rather than what He actually asked for.

COMMANDS VERSUS EXPECTATIONS

There is a simple exercise I walk through with church leaders. First, I have them list all the things that people expect from their church. They usually list obvious things like a really good service, strong age-specific ministries, a certain style/volume/length of singing, a well-communicated sermon, conveniences such as parking, a clean church building, coffee, childcare, etc. Then I have them list the commands God gave the Church in Scripture. Usually they mention commands like "love one another as I have loved you" (John 15:12), "visit orphans and widows in their affliction" (James 1:27), "make disciples of all nations" (Matt. 28:19), "bear one another's burdens" (Gal. 6:2), etc. I then ask them what would upset their people more—if the church didn't provide the things from the first list or if the church didn't obey the commands in the second list.

In Luke 12, Jesus told a parable about a master leaving his servants with specific tasks. When the master returned, he expected to see the tasks accomplished. When he saw his commands neglected, the servants were punished harshly. How can we shrug our shoulders at a parable like this? That's insane! Jesus is returning soon, and He expects to find His Church taking His commands seriously. Yet far too often we are more concerned with how well the sermon was communicated, whether the youth group is relevant enough, or how to make the music better. Honestly, what is it that gets people in your church stirred up for change? Is it disobedience toward commands from God? Or is it falling short of expectations that we have made up? The answer to these questions might just show us whether our church exists to please God or please people— whether God is leading our church or we are.

Jesus was eating with His disciples in Mark 7 when some Pharisees called out His disciples for not washing their hands. This was a strong tradition of the elders that all Jews observed by washing before eating (v. 3). They treated it as a major offense, as though God was really upset if someone didn't wash, but the problem was this: God never commanded people to wash their hands before they eat. There is no reason to think God cares all that much about it, especially in comparison with all the things He has commanded.

Jesus responded by calling them hypocrites and saying they were "teaching as doctrines the commandments of men," that they "leave the commandment of God and hold to the tradition of men," and finally accused them of having "a fine way of rejecting the commandment of God in order to establish your tradition" (vv. 7–9). Jesus was really upset about this!

God had given clear commands in the Old Testament He expected His people to obey (613 things to be exact). Then along the way those people created additional traditions God never actually asked them to do but they felt were good ideas. Washing hands and dishes before eating is one example. It wasn't wrong for them to do it. It's actually a great idea. That's not why Jesus called them hypocrites. He rebuked them so harshly because they had created their own traditions to obey (which aren't important) and emphasized them more than the actual commands God had given them (which are extremely important).

Honoring traditions made the Pharisees feel like they were obeying God when they actually weren't. If we are not careful, we can be guilty of the same sin resulting in the same divine displeasure.

Many of us have become so accustomed to various traditions that we genuinely think they are commanded. I have seen people become furious over the absence of Sunday school while being indifferent toward the absence of the Lord's Supper. Some rant over the style of music while shrugging their shoulders at the neglect of widows and orphans in their distress. It may surprise some of you that a forty-minute sermon isn't commanded but "bear one another's burdens, and so fulfill the law of Christ" is actually in the Bible (Gal. 6:2). I could go on and on about how those who complain about dress, youth ministry, and service times are also the same people who have not shared their faith in months (or years) and couldn't care less about making disciples of the billions of people who have no idea who Jesus is!

It is imperative that we differentiate between what we want and what God commands. Not that our desires are all bad, but they must take a back seat to what He emphasizes.

WHAT WORKS

I have been in church leadership for thirty years. I spent years asking myself, "What will work?" And by that I meant, "What will get more people to attend gatherings?" This isn't necessarily a bad thing. My intention was that I wanted more people interested in Christ, and I wanted to see their lives changed. In my zeal for results, however, I neglected some of His commands. Paul didn't do this. If you read Romans 9:1–3, you see that Paul was far more zealous for the salvation of others than any of us. Yet in his pursuit of people, he was still careful to guard what was sacred.

Paul was careful to refrain from using merely human rhetoric and make sure the Spirit's power was predominant. I was busy doing whatever worked. I learned how to keep an auditorium filled. I learned how to give people the experience they wanted.

Paul rose above all this. The Corinthians wanted Paul to preach with eloquence like the skilled orators they enjoyed listening to, but Paul refused (1 Cor. 1:17). They wanted a preacher who would give them the best of human wisdom, but Paul gave them the opposite. He actually limited his words because he didn't want to diminish the cross of its power. He wanted their faith to rest on the Spirit's power (2:1–5). They wanted a Christian celebrity they could all praise (2 Cor. 11), but Paul refused to let it be about him. He gave them what they needed and what was best for them rather than what they were demanding.

> *"For Christ did not send me to baptize but to preach*
> *the gospel, and not with words of eloquent wisdom,*
> *lest the cross of Christ be emptied of its power."*
>
> 1 Corinthians 1:17

> *"And I, when I came to you, brothers, did not come*
> *proclaiming to you the testimony of God with lofty*
> *speech or wisdom. For I decided to know nothing*
> *among you except Jesus Christ and him crucified. And*
> *I was with you in weakness and in fear and much*
> *trembling, and my speech and my message were not in*
> *plausible words of wisdom, but in demonstration of*
> *the Spirit and of power, so that your faith might not*
> *rest in the wisdom of men but in the power of God."*
>
> 1 Corinthians 2:1–5

As long as I have been alive, church attendance has been in decline (compared with overall population growth).[1] So it's not surprising to see well-intentioned pastors trying to make the Church more popular. But this is actually an old game that has never worked out well. In nineteenth-century Denmark, Søren Kierkegaard was appalled at the state church, which he believed had grown apathetic and insincere. Kierkegaard believed that true Christianity is costly and demands humility. Because the gospel exposes our failures and insists that we can find life only through the grace of God, our self-esteem comes under attack as we acknowledge that Jesus alone saves. But what Kierkegaard saw in the Church were constant attempts to make Christianity more palatable, more popular, and less offensive. He said if we strip away the offense from Christianity and try to make things fun and easy for everyone, "then lock the churches, the sooner the better, or turn them into places of amusement which stand open all day long!"[2]

Does that sound pertinent for today?

Alan Hirsch explained his experience with building a megachurch in Australia: "If you have to use marketing and the lures of entertainment to attract people, then you will have to keep them there on the [same] principle because that is what people buy in to.… Win them with entertainment, and you have to keep them there by entertaining them. For a whole lot of reasons, this commitment seems to get harder year after year. We end up creating a whip for our own backs."[3]

If we focus too much of our attention on what people want, we will only increase the amount of complaining. The more we try to fulfill their desires, the more they complain when their desires are not met. Now we have many people who genuinely believe their unhappiness is the church's fault! Much of the fault lies with leaders like me for addressing these problems the wrong way.

If it's 11:00 p.m. and your ten-year-old asks for a latte because he's tired, you need to tell him to go to sleep. Sleep is the right solution for his fatigue. Too often we have given people what they ask for rather than what they need. There are times when the most loving thing we can do is teach people that joy will come only when they stop screaming for attention and save their voices for the throne.

> *"Then I looked, and I heard around the throne and the living creatures and the elders the voice of many angels, numbering myriads of myriads and thousands of thousands, saying with a loud voice, 'Worthy is the Lamb who was slain, to receive power and wealth and wisdom and might and honor and glory and blessing!' And I heard every creature in heaven and on earth and under the earth and in the sea, and all that is in them, saying, 'To him who sits on the throne and to the Lamb be blessing and honor and glory and might forever and ever!' And the four living creatures said, 'Amen!' and the elders fell down and worshiped."*
>
> Revelation 5:11–14

Can you imagine being in that setting and feeling bored? Feeling like you needed something more? Wishing people were being more attentive to your needs? There's no way! This is what we were made for! We're not doing people any favors by pretending they are the center of the universe. Either people will be awed by the sacred or they will not. If the sacred is not enough, then it is clear that the Spirit has not done a work in their lives. If the sheep don't hear His voice, let them walk away. Don't call out with your own voice.

Too often we add in our own voices, thinking if we offer just the right services or package the gospel in just the right way so no one gets offended, we can convince people to stay. By catering our worship to the worshippers and not to the Object of our worship, I fear we have created human-centered churches.

I don't say this to condemn anyone or to point any fingers. I am guilty of it too. When I look back at my life and the times when I fell prey to this consumerist mentality, I don't believe that my intentions were evil or that my love for Christ was weak. God may say otherwise in the end, but I really believe my biggest mistake was that I didn't think things through. Or that I didn't consult the right Person enough. I got caught up in consumerism like everyone else, and I paid too much attention to what I wanted and what others wanted.

Many of us make decisions based on what brings us the most pleasure. This is how we choose our homes, jobs, cars, clothes, food, and churches. We pursue what we want; then we make sure there are no biblical commands we are violating. In essence, we want to know what God will tolerate rather than what He desires. Maybe we are afraid to ask what will bring Him the most pleasure. Ignorance feels better than disobedience.

The good news is that by the grace of God, some of us are seeing our failures now and are training ourselves to prioritize His desires. Scripture is our starting point, not desire or tradition. Rather than thinking of what we would enjoy or asking others what they would like, we ask the simple question, What would please God most?

DEVOTED TO HIS ORDERS

The first church was built on the things that pleased God most. It was their focus on the right things that actually made them attractive. You can't read through the book of Acts without thinking, *That's a community of people I want to be part of.* What they were doing was unique. It was compelling in a way that nothing else in the world could rival. This was something the world had never seen.

> *"And they devoted themselves to the apostles' teaching and the fellowship, to the breaking of bread and the prayers. And awe came upon every soul, and many wonders and signs were being done through the apostles. And all who believed were together and had all things in common. And they were selling their possessions and belongings and distributing the proceeds to all, as any*

had need. And day by day, attending the temple together
and breaking bread in their homes, they received their
food with glad and generous hearts, praising God and
having favor with all the people. And the Lord added to
their number day by day those who were being saved."

Acts 2:42–47

Absent from this account is any attempt on the part of the early Christians to conjure up some sort of powerful experience. They weren't strategizing ways to get people interested. After Jesus left them to return to His Father, they were gathering together to ask God to direct them and work through them: "All these with one accord were devoting themselves to prayer" (Acts 1:14). It was in one of these gatherings that the Spirit of God descended on them and the entire Church was launched as they "devoted themselves to the apostles' teaching and the fellowship, to the breaking of bread and the prayers" (2:42).

No modern church-growth movement would take this approach seriously. Where's the excitement? Sure, these elements are the basic building blocks, but do you really think you can accomplish anything with just the apostles' teaching, fellowship, breaking of bread, and prayer? After all, haven't there been many who have chased this simple approach without experiencing the "awe" the early church felt? No. There's a keyword in this passage that separates the attempts of our modern church from the first church: *devoted*.

In our impatient culture, we want to experience biblical awe without biblical devotion. At the core of our dysfunction is not necessarily style or structure but lack of devotion. So much of the discussion nowadays revolves around how to make the most of our Sunday morning services. If people are willing to sacrifice ninety minutes a week, should we spend that time singing, preaching, or praying? Should we meet in a large group or a small one? These are all the wrong questions. We should be asking why Christians are willing to give only ninety minutes a week (if that!) to the only thing that really matters in their lives! So leaders work tirelessly to squeeze prayer, teaching, fellowship, and Communion into a ninety-minute service because they believe that's all they have to work with.

While we can't force people to be devoted, it may be that we have made it too easy for them not to be. By trying to keep everyone interested and excited, we've created a cheap substitute for devotion.

Rather than busying themselves with countless endeavors, the early followers devoted themselves to a few. And it changed the world. It seems like the Church in America is constantly looking for the next new thing. We want to follow the latest trends of church growth, believing there is something we are missing. Once we add one more staff position or one more program, our churches will become healthy. It's a never-ending game. Haven't we tried that long enough?

THE APOSTLES' TEACHING

The early church devoted themselves to the apostles' teaching. There is a miraculous power to the apostles' teaching that no other writings have (Eph. 2:20; 2 Tim. 3:16–17). Most Christians have heard all their lives that "the word of God is living and active, sharper than any two-edged sword, piercing to the division of soul and of spirit, of joints and of marrow, and discerning the thoughts and intentions of the heart" (Heb. 4:12). We've heard it, but do we believe it?

If we genuinely believed that the Word of God was this powerful, what would we do? We would read these words and expect them to have a life of their own. We certainly wouldn't put so much emphasis on different preachers and their ability to "make the Scriptures come alive"!

Think of movies you've seen where a witch recites a spell. Everything has to be repeated exactly, because the power comes from the words themselves. Obviously, I'm not trying to compare the Word of God to a spell book, but if anything, we should treat these words as more sacred and powerful, not less.

"It is the Spirit who gives life; the flesh
is no help at all. The words that I have
spoken to you are spirit and life."

John 6:63

If I was at the park playing basketball and LeBron James wanted to play on my team, I'd find every opportunity to pass him the ball. Then I would stand back and watch in amazement. What if we spent more time publicly reading the Word and encouraging others to read it too? I suspect we would be able to sit back and watch in amazement as the Word of God accomplishes what it sets out to do.

> *"For as the rain and the snow come down from*
> *heaven and do not return there but water the earth,*
> *making it bring forth and sprout, giving seed to the*
> *sower and bread to the eater, so shall my word be that*
> *goes out from my mouth; it shall not return to me*
> *empty, but it shall accomplish that which I purpose,*
> *and shall succeed in the thing for which I sent it."*
> Isaiah 55:10–11

My preaching habits over the years have shown that I believe His words are dead and require my creativity to bring them to life. Paul said, "Devote yourself to the public reading of Scripture" (1 Tim. 4:13). Maybe if we did more of this, we could raise a new generation that is addicted to God's Word and less fanatical about preachers.

A friend of mine gathered some people for a time of public Bible reading. They read in shifts, starting at Genesis 1 and finishing with Revelation 22 three days later. In seventy-two hours, they read the entire Bible aloud! He tried to describe the feeling they had when the final words were read. Ultimately, it was unexplainable. The Word did something that far exceeded their expectations. They did in three days what most professing Christians in America won't do in their lifetimes.

What would it mean for us to strip away the distractions and become a people who devoted ourselves to Scripture? I firmly believe that we would see a power in our churches like we've never experienced before.

Just a few weeks ago, at our church gathering we read the entire book of Revelation out loud. I started by reading Revelation 1:3: "Blessed is the one who reads aloud the words of this prophecy, and blessed are those who hear, and who keep what is written in it, for the time is near."

Isn't it ridiculous that God promises a blessing to anyone who reads Revelation out loud yet no one actually does this? So we took turns reading a chapter each until all twenty-two chapters were read. It was powerful. The Word of God read simply and without embellishment brought us to a deeper and purer form of worship than anything I could have said.

We have all seen videos of people in Third-World countries washing their clothes in dirty water. While it might be better than not washing them at all, they're not actually clean. That is how I feel like my preaching can be. It's certainly better than nothing, but my words will always be dirty compared with the purity of the Word of God. Only His Word is unstained by the world. It is the only thing with the power to cleanse us thoroughly. If we really want to come before God with clean hands and pure hearts, we need to have a greater awe and longing for His Word alone.

THE BREAKING OF BREAD

The first disciples devoted themselves to the breaking of bread, which in the New Testament refers to a shared meal in which they celebrated the Lord's Supper. Think of what this would have been like for them. Jesus had a profound impact on all the people in the early church. His sacrificial death on the cross and subsequent resurrection were real for them. They were misunderstood and opposed by the people around them; some were beaten or even put to death for following Jesus.

So imagine what it would have meant to them when they gathered with the few people who shared their mission and beliefs. Imagine sitting around a table and sharing a meal with people who loved you unconditionally and whose lives had changed in the same way as yours. As you gather, you can't help but remember those who used to sit at the table with you but were killed for proclaiming His death. Some who gather with you have injuries and scars from the persecution. You break the bread and eat it, remembering that Jesus had broken His body so you could find life in Him. Imagine drinking wine with these fellow believers as you recall how His blood was shed. He did this for you so you could be cleansed and forgiven of all your sins. Can you see how powerful this experience would have been for the church every time they gathered?

If Communion has become boring for us now, it could be that we've lost sight of the value of Jesus' sacrifice. When Communion feels like an obligation rather than a life-giving necessity, a serious heart scan needs to take place. God wants us to love the Lord's Supper so much that we feel as if we can't live without it! Have you ever felt this way, or have you allowed the broken body and shed blood of Jesus to become just another theological concept?

God designed Communion to be an intimate act of remembering His flesh and blood. More than just an exercise of the mind, He wanted us to actually eat of the bread and drink of the cup. And Communion is not just about intimacy with Jesus; it's also about intimacy with one another. Remember that Jesus had just washed the disciples' feet and commanded them to love one another *just as* He loved them. It was after this that He taught them to stare at His broken body and blood to remind them of how He loved them. As we consider the cross and look around the room, we should be asking ourselves, "Am I willing to love the people in this room to that extent?" This probably sounds impossible to most churchgoers, yet it's what Christ asks for. Just imagine if the Church was made up of people who would literally go to the cross for one another. How could people shrug their shoulders as they witnessed that kind of love? This is what unbelievers should see when they watch us break bread with one another. If Communion feels like a curious add-on to our church services rather than the very core of everything we're about, then we're missing the point of the Church.

THE FELLOWSHIP

As the Spirit of God empowered the Church, they devoted themselves to the fellowship. They had a dedication to one another that would be impossible unless God was in their midst. This is not something to take lightly. In fact, the whole next chapter of this book is devoted to this concept. So let's pause on fellowship and move on to the next element.

THE PRAYERS

Do you remember the last time you gathered with believers just to pray? Or is prayer something you do only before you eat or something your church does only when it needs to transition out of the sermon while the band walks onto the stage?

Would you say that prayer plays any meaningful role in the life of your church? If prayer isn't vital for your church, then your church isn't vital. This statement may be bold, but I believe it's true. If you can accomplish your church's mission without daily, passionate prayer, then your mission is insufficient and your church is irrelevant.

The early church devoted themselves to prayer. They knew they couldn't exist without it. If God didn't come through, they could never fulfill the mission He had given them. So they were constantly on their knees together.

> *"And when they had prayed, the place in which*
> *they were gathered together was shaken, and they*
> *were all filled with the Holy Spirit and continued*
> *to speak the word of God with boldness."*
>
> Acts 4:31

In Acts 4, the early Christians had just prayed for signs and wonders and boldness. Immediately after, the ground shook and they left in boldness! Don't you at least want to try this? Don't "church activities" sound pretty boring in comparison? How can we read about the experience of the early church as they prayed and then settle for energetic services? I believe there is something deep in you that would love to pray intensely with like-minded people, hoping to see a supernatural response.

A BETTER EXPERIENCE

God commands the Church to be devoted to His Word, to fellowship, to the Lord's Supper, and to prayer. Why? Because God desires His people to experience *Him*. He who is infinitely greater than anything we could ever imagine—the Creator of the universe—desires intimacy with us. He has given us a road map for seeking and finding Him, and we have forsaken it because we think we have better ideas. Can you see how absurd that is?

Our job is to reveal God to people. He is present in His Word, fellowship, Communion, and prayer. Rather than creating our own pep rallies, our calling is to simply put Him on display and watch as He draws people to Himself. If they are not interested in Him, what do we think we're accomplishing by trying to lure them by other means? We have to accept the fact that not everyone is interested in God. We just need to make sure that it's really God we are putting on display. Otherwise we run the risk of people attending our services who have merely fallen in love with us.

THE PARTY

I asked my daughter how many kids would come to her birthday party if all we offered was cake. No games, no entertainment. They could come to the house to spend time with her and bring gifts to celebrate her, but we wouldn't have anything else for them. She thought for a minute and said, "Maybe just a couple." Then I asked her how many would come if I rented out Dave & Buster's and let them have unlimited tokens, food, and prizes. She laughed and said confidently that the whole school would show up.

So let's say that for her birthday party I rent out the arcade and her whole school comes. They're all going nuts, having the time of their lives. Imagine if I pulled her aside during the party, put my arm around her, and said, "Look at all the people who came to be with you!" Would she actually believe those people were there because they love her and want to spend time with her? Or would my comment actually be insulting?

Isn't this basically what we do with God? We have learned that we can fill church buildings if we bring in the right speaker or band. Make things exciting enough and people will come. We say, "God, look how many people are coming because they love being with You!" But do we really think God is fooled by this? Do we think God is pleased? He knows how many would show up if it was just Him. He knows there might be only a few if all we offered was Communion or prayer.

Most of us do this out of good motives, I think. We are just trying to get people to show up to His party. But based on everything you read in Scripture, does that seem like what Jesus would want? Again, if God had it His way, would He really want a bunch of churches desperate to entertain? Or would He want to be the reason people were coming, even if that meant a much smaller number of people? On top of that, are we sure what Jesus is looking for is well-attended church services? Our current models seem directed at this and little else. Mike Breen said, "Most of us have become quite good at the church thing.

And yet, disciples are the only thing that Jesus cares about, and it's the only number that Jesus is counting. Not our attendance or budget or buildings."[4]

In the book of Malachi, God's people had become bored with worship. God's response was not mild. As the prophet Malachi called them back to the passion, devotion, and sacrifice of true worship, the people responded by saying, "What a weariness this is" (Mal. 1:13). They saw worship not as an honor but as an obligation. Today we'd respond to this by saying, "Look at how bored they are! Let's make worship more exciting; then people will really get something out of it!"

But God's response was much different. He was so offended by it all that He would rather they simply shut the whole thing down.

> *"Oh that there were one among you who would*
> *shut the doors, that you might not kindle fire on*
> *my altar in vain! I have no pleasure in you, says*
> *the LORD of hosts, and I will not accept an offering*
> *from your hand. For from the rising of the sun to its*
> *setting my name will be great among the nations,*
> *and in every place incense will be offered to my*
> *name, and a pure offering. For my name will be*
> *great among the nations, says the LORD of hosts."*
>
> Malachi 1:10–11

Stop the game. Shut the doors. This whole thing is an insult (see 2:3).

Years ago, my friend from India drove me to a speaking engagement in Dallas. When he heard the music and saw the lights, he said, "You Americans are funny. You won't show up unless there's a good speaker or band. In India, people get excited just to pray." He proceeded to tell me how believers back home love Communion and how they flock to simple prayer gatherings. I imagined God looking down on the earth and seeing people on one side of the planet gathering expectantly whenever prayer was happening. Meanwhile, on the other side of the planet, people show up only for the most talented people and the "atmosphere." It's embarrassing.

David Platt echoed this: "I am also struck by our reliance upon having just the right speaker and just the right musician who can attract the most people to a worship service. But what if the church itself—the people of God gathered in one place—is intended to be the attraction, regardless of who is teaching or singing that day? This is enough for our brothers and sisters around the world."[5]

Just as God said through Malachi, there will always be those who will worship Him wholeheartedly. He's not desperate.

However, it is His desire for all His children to experience the fullness of Him through the Church, and He has given us His Word to show us how.

Let's dream of trembling believers on their knees, speechless because they grasp the weight of speaking to Yahweh. Let's picture small groups and large crowds coming with eager expectation, just to pray. This is possible, even in America.

Dream of people going house to house to take Communion. Some spontaneously bursting into tears, others bursting into song, no one indifferent. One person praises God for His sacrifice, imagining the Father's pain as Christ's blood flowed. Another sits speechless, stunned by the intimacy of eating His flesh and drinking His blood. Another shouts for joy as he experiences the complete cleansing of his darkest sins.

Dream of groups that tremble as Scripture is read. People are on the edge of their seats, giving God's words the honor they deserve. It matters little who is reading. It is the Bible they find riveting. Explanations are given when needed, but people are mainly listening for truth so they can repent and worship.

Dream of true fellowship where people are living in perfect harmony with God and one another. A picture of Eden where God and humans are walking side by side. Christ is at the center of all relationships; picture Him bringing together people who are very different as they marvel at Him together, as they do in heaven.

4

THE GANG

We live in a time when people go to a building on Sunday mornings, attend an hour-long service, and call themselves members of the Church.

Does that sound shocking to you? Of course not. This is perfectly normal. It's what we grew up with. We all know good Christians go to church.

But have you ever read the New Testament? Do you find anything in Scripture that is even remotely close to the pattern we have created? Do you find anyone who "went" to church?

Try to imagine Paul and Peter speaking like we do today: "Hey, Peter, where do you go to church now?"

"I go to The River. They have great music and I love the kids' program."

"Cool. Can I check out your church next Sunday? I'm not getting much out of mine."

"Totally. I'm not going to be there next Sunday because little Matthew has soccer. But how about the week after?"

"Sounds good. Hey, do they have a singles' group?"

It's comical to think of Paul and Peter speaking like this. Yet that's a normal conversation among Christians today. Why? There are so many things wrong with the above conversation I don't even know where to start. The fact that we have reduced the sacred mystery of Church to a one-hour service we attend is staggering. Yet that's the way I defined it for years! I didn't know anything different. It's what everyone did, so I didn't think to question it.

LET'S GO TO GANG

Think about it this way. One of the elders of my church, Rob, spent most of his life in gangs. He encountered Jesus when he was imprisoned and placed in solitary confinement. Today he is one of the most loving people I know. In fact, I'm not sure I know of anyone who loves Jesus and people as well as he does.

Rob tells me stories of gang life and the fear he felt when he left his gang to join the body of Christ. To do this in prison can be suicidal; he had to make a serious break with his gang, and gangs are anything but casual about breaking those ties. But the Lord intervened to spare his life. It wasn't just the physical torture or death he feared; he dreaded the rejection by those he loved. The gang was his family. These were loyal and dear friends who looked out for him twenty-four hours a day. There was a love and camaraderie from being in a gang that he had enjoyed since childhood. Now he would lose those relationships and be hated by them all.

When Rob describes gang life, much of it sounds like what the Church was meant to be. Obviously, there are major differences (drugs, murder—you know, little details like that), but the idea of "being a family" is central to both gang life and God's design for the Church. Yet while we use family terminology in our churches, Rob's stories have convinced me that the gangs have a much stronger sense of what it means to be a family than we do in the Church.

From what you know about gangs, could you ever imagine gang life being reduced to a weekly one-hour gathering? No group would meet briefly once a week and call that a gang. Imagine one gang member walking up to another one and saying, "Yo, how was gang? I had to miss this week because life has been crazy!"

We all know enough about gangs to know that's ridiculous. Yet every week we hear Christians asking each other, "How was church?" Something that God has designed to function as a family has been reduced to an optional weekly meeting. And this has become normal. Expected. How in the world did we get here? Any gang member will tell you his homies have his back. They're there for him. They're loyal, committed, present. Meanwhile, in many churches, you have about as much of a connection to the people who are supposedly your spiritual family as you would to someone who visited the same movie theater as you.

SUPERNATURAL LOVE

Is it just a nice cliché to say the Church should be like a family? I mean, it's a great thought, but our *families* are our families! Does God really expect us to be this close with people we're not related to, people we wouldn't even choose to be friends with? I agree that it's natural to be close with your family and unnatural to experience this with people who are not like you. But that's exactly the point! It's not supposed to be natural—it's supernatural!

> *"A new commandment I give to you, that you love one another: just as I have loved you, you also are to love one another. By this all people will know that you are my disciples, if you have love for one another."*
>
> John 13:34–35

One thing the New Testament makes clear is that the Church is supposed to be known for its love. Jesus says our love for one another is the very thing that will attract the world. But can you name a single church in our country that is known for the way its members love one another? I'm sure you can think of churches known for excitement or powerful preaching or worship or production value. But can you name a church known for supernatural love?

When the phrase "one another" is mentioned over a hundred times in the New Testament (love one another, care for …, pray for …, admonish …, etc.), why is it that you can't think of a single church known for the way they take care of one another? God clearly cares about this. Why don't we? As elders at Cornerstone Church, we asked ourselves whether people would notice supernatural love when they walked into our gatherings. It was not that we were void of love; it just didn't stand out. Honestly, the love in our midst was a far cry from anything that we could attribute to the Holy Spirit.

At this point, some of you are probably thinking, *Well, that's Francis's experience with his church. I'm actually part of a very loving congregation, probably more loving than what he experienced at Cornerstone.* It's possible, but you need to know that Cornerstone was a very loving church, as far as American churches go. We really enjoyed being with one another, had some good small groups, and served the poor in our area and around the world. We were a very nice and kind church, and we definitely witnessed some Spirit-inspired acts of love. With some notable exceptions, we just weren't experiencing what we saw in the Bible.

As elders, we weren't content to just love people better than the church down the street. We were looking for biblical love. Our love felt too similar to the love we received from coworkers and neighbors. Sometimes we are too quick to label our church experience as "Christian love." Jesus made it clear that even sinners know how to love one another (Luke 6:32–34). Haven't you ever worked in a restaurant, joined a gym, or bonded with other parents at your kids' sporting events? Is the love you experience in your church really that different? It's supposed to be.

Jesus said, "As I have loved you, you also are to love one another" (John 13:34). Our King, who allowed Himself to be tortured and killed for us, tells us to love one another in the same way. Have you ever even considered loving a fellow Christian as sacrificially and selflessly as Christ loved you? When was the last time you looked at a Christian brother or sister selflessly, wanting to bring him or her life no matter what the cost?

Think of a few of the people in your church. Picture their faces. Now think about the lengths to which Jesus went to bring those specific people to Himself. Think of the whippings He endured so that they could be forgiven. Imagine the way He thought of each of those people as He hung on the cross.

No sacrifice was too great; there was nothing He would hold back. He did everything necessary to redeem and heal and transform those specific people.

He did the same for you. So ask yourself, Who does God want you to pursue? Who could you desire to spend time with more? Jesus went to the ultimate extent for them; why would you hold anything back? Jesus pursued those people from heaven to earth to bring them into His family; what barriers could hold you back from pursuing a deep familial relationship with them?

We have experienced the greatest love in the universe. Shouldn't that profound love flow out of us? And shouldn't that be enough to shock the world?

> *"Beloved, let us love one another, for love is from God,*
> *and whoever loves has been born of God and knows*
> *God. Anyone who does not love does not know God,*
> *because God is love. In this the love of God was made*
> *manifest among us, that God sent his only Son into*
> *the world, so that we might live through him. In this*
> *is love, not that we have loved God but that he loved*
> *us and sent his Son to be the propitiation for our sins.*
> *Beloved, if God so loved us, we also ought to love one*
> *another. No one has ever seen God; if we love one another,*
> *God abides in us and his love is perfected in us."*
>
> 1 John 4:7–12

Did you catch that? Right there is a promise that *if we love one another*, God will *abide* in us and His love will be *perfected* in us. Is there anything in the world you want more than that? We don't live like this statement is true. And that breaks my heart, because there is also a serious warning in this passage that those who don't love don't know God. What does this say about our churches? The importance of loving one another is emphasized all throughout Scripture (Rom. 12:9–10; 1 Cor. 13; 1 Pet. 4:8; etc.), and I can't help feeling as if we're missing out on something extraordinary because of our lack of love.

SUPERNATURAL UNITY

When Jesus was approaching the cross, He prayed a fascinating prayer. This prayer was for His disciples, and some of His statements have really challenged my faith.

> *"I do not ask for these only, but also for those who will believe in me through their word, that they may all be one, just as you, Father, are in me, and I in you, that they also may be in us, so that the world may believe that you have sent me. The glory that you have given me I have given to them, that they may be one even as we are one, I in them and you in me, that they may*

become perfectly one, so that the world may know that
you sent me and loved them even as you loved me."
John 17:20–23

Jesus prayed that the unity of His followers would be equal to the oneness of the Father and Son! He wants you and me to be one *just as* the Father and Son are united. Have you ever considered pursuing this type of unity with your church?

Do you even believe this is possible?

Let me keep going with this. Jesus' prayer was not that we would just get along and avoid church splits. His prayer was that we would become "perfectly one." He prayed this because our oneness was designed to be the way to prove that Jesus was the Messiah. Jesus said the purpose of our unity was *"so that the world may know that you sent me and loved them."*

For some of us, that prayer doesn't make sense. How could our unity result in the world's belief? How could seeing us love one another make someone believe that Jesus truly came from heaven? It feels like saying two plus two equals a thousand. Just remember that Scripture is filled with impossible equations. Marching around a city seven times doesn't seem as if it would result in its walls collapsing, but then it happened (Josh. 6). Church unity doesn't seem as if it would result in people getting saved, but it actually did happen (Acts 2:44–47).

They were united and the result was people being saved. Acts describes the extent of their unity like this:

> *"Now the full number of those who believed were of*
> *one heart and soul, and no one said that any of the*
> *things that belonged to him was his own, but they had*
> *everything in common. And with great power the apostles*
> *were giving their testimony to the resurrection of the*
> *Lord Jesus, and great grace was upon them all. There*
> *was not a needy person among them, for as many as*
> *were owners of lands or houses sold them and brought*
> *the proceeds of what was sold and laid it at the apostles'*
> *feet, and it was distributed to each as any had need."*
>
> Acts 4:32–35

I don't know about you, but that passage always moves me. The Church looks so beautiful, so attractive. It is that kind of love that makes our message believable. Scripture is clear: there is a real connection between our unity and the believability of our message. If we are serious about winning the lost, we must be serious about pursuing unity.

> *"Only let your manner of life be worthy of the gospel*
> *of Christ, so that whether I come and see you or am*
> *absent, I may hear of you that you are standing firm*
> *in one spirit, with one mind striving side by side for*

the faith of the gospel, and not frightened in anything
by your opponents. This is a clear sign to them of their
destruction, but of your salvation, and that from God."
Philippians 1:27–28

If you skipped past the verses above, please go back and read them. Then read them again. Notice the promise at the end: our fearless unity is "a clear sign to [those who oppose Christians] of their destruction"! We are living in a time when very few people believe in the wrath of God. Even the evilest people we know have no fear of a literal judgment day. Have you ever tried to convince someone of their future destruction? It's not a simple task. Yet Scripture tells us that our fearless unity will convince them.

When are we going to take these promises seriously and spend our energy seeking unity? Not just the kind of unity where we avoid arguments with one another, but the kind where we truly live together as a family. Where we meet one another's needs and care for one another regardless of the time or effort required. Unity doesn't come easily. Think of everything it takes for a family to stay together—all the acts of service it requires, all the forgiveness and grace that must be constantly extended, all the times when one person's desires have to be lovingly laid aside for the desires of others. It's easy to talk about unity, but it requires a kind of mutual commitment that is all but absent from our churches. If we're going to see this become a reality, we need to count the cost and decide whether we will commit. I don't know about you, but this doesn't come naturally to me. I'm an introvert who is happy with a few close friends. Obedience often grates against our natural desires, but if we obey only when it feels natural, then Jesus is not truly Lord of our lives. What often results from obedience, however, is unexpected blessing. Now that I am starting to experience true unity with my brothers and sisters, I don't want to ever live without it.

Pushing the Church to live as a family is not some gimmick, some flavor of "church" that would be fun to try; it's commanded. And it's offered. Crafting the Church into a truly united and supernaturally loving family is the very thing God is wanting to do. Do we believe God is capable? Do we trust that His design for His Church is what will be most effective?

We have come up with countless strategies to reach the lost when God promises that unity is the method that will work. Think about that: God gave us instructions on how to reach the world, yet we abandon the one set of instructions He gave us even as we scramble to create classes and programs and events that promote everything but the strategy God gave us!

HAVE WE GIVEN UP?

When you read about the unity of the early church, does it make you jealous? Something in you wishes you were born two thousand years ago so you could be a part of a group like this. You can get depressed by the dual realization that this is the very thing you've always wanted and you're not going to find this in the typical American church today.

It's sad that our churches look nothing like this. It's devastating that we don't believe it is possible.

What I see today is many people choosing to opt out of the Church. Claiming a continued love for Jesus, they have decided that the Church only gets in their way. It's a sad time when those who want to be close to Jesus have given up on the Church.

There is this terrifying verse in 1 Timothy where Paul talked about two men who rejected the faith. Paul said that he had handed them over to Satan, by which he meant that he'd put them outside the Church (1:20). Basically, these men were actively opposing the works of God, so rather than pretending everything was fine, Paul removed them from the safety and blessings of the fellowship of believers. He was hoping that the misery of being separated from the Church would lead them to repent. Are you catching the weight of this? Paul equated removal from the Church with being handed over to Satan! It is crazy to me that we live in a time when people are voluntarily doing this to themselves! No church has placed them outside the fellowship; instead, they've handed themselves over to Satan!

Real love, unity, and blessing were supposed to be found in the Church. Many are having a hard time finding that, so they're setting off on their own. Jesus said that the world would see the supernatural unity and love we share in the Church and believe in Him through that. But we're not experiencing it. We've given up on it. We no longer believe it is possible.

What if we took God's description of the Church as a family seriously? What would happen if a group of people sought Jesus fervently, loved one another sacrificially, and then shared the gospel boldly?

Sadly, there are a lot of people in our churches who aren't interested in living out loving family like this. I'm going to say something that might be hard to hear: What if we let them leave? I know that goes against all the wisdom of modern church-growth strategies, but it's exactly the kind of thing Jesus would do. While we design strategies to slowly ease people into Christian commitment and grow attendance at our services, Jesus called people to count the cost from the very start (Luke 14:25–35). He didn't expect His followers to be perfect, but He did demand that they be committed (Luke 9:57–62). The people who leave your church because they're turned off by the level of relational commitment will find another church that can provide what they're looking for. You can't shape the life of your church around who might leave if things start to feel too much like the New Testament.

Jesus didn't sugarcoat anything, but He did promise that His Spirit can bind us together in a way we've never experienced. Maybe we've just been so distracted by our efforts to make our church services exciting that we've hardly noticed the people the Spirit wants to unite us with.

What if we followed God's design for the Church and in doing so allowed the Church to be pruned down to only those who wanted to obey His command to "love one another as I have loved you" (John 15:12)? We might actually find that a pruned tree would bear more fruit (v. 2). We might discover that the branches that weren't bearing fruit were actually sucking all the life out of the tree.

Don't forget that there are times when God doesn't just want us to let them leave; He wants us to ask them to. There is a difficult reality to face, which is that there are going to be people who try to take advantage of churches that are committed to love. In order to love one another like family, we will need to have grace and forgiveness. However, sometimes the most loving thing to do for people is not to enable them in their sin but to follow the aforementioned example of Paul in 1 Timothy, who separated people from the Church. It was for the good of the Church as well as the individuals who were removed. Biblical unity is achieved not by overlooking sin but through firm pruning, which can lead to repentance. Unconditional love doesn't always look the way we expect it to. It takes tremendous love to risk rejection for the hope of loving a sinner to repentance.

BE ENCOURAGED

For years I honestly didn't have faith that it was even possible for a church to possess the love and unity I saw in Scripture. People kept telling me this couldn't happen in America. I would see examples of this in places like China, but church leaders would tell me it worked there only because people already lived communally and because they were experiencing persecution that forced them to bond. There was always a part of me that doubted those voices, but it was only a few years ago that I mustered up the courage to try. It was harder than I expected, but it's also been more rewarding than I could have dreamed. This can happen wherever you are too. Holy Spirit love and unity are not confined to persecuted countries.

5

SERVANTS

How would you respond if Jesus took off your shoes right now and began to wash your feet? Try to envision this.

I wouldn't be able to hold it together. I picture myself crying uncontrollably. I think I would feel so unworthy and uncomfortable but also secure and honored. I can barely imagine standing in the same room as Jesus. My mind doesn't have a compartment that fits the thought of my Creator and Judge washing my feet. It feels impossible.

At the core of our faith lies this belief that almighty God humbled Himself to serve us and die for us. At the root of our calling is a command to imitate Him by serving one another. After washing the disciples' feet, Jesus commanded them to wash one another's feet (John 13:14). Yet on any given Sunday, what percentage of "Christians" show up eager to serve others?

> *"The Son of Man came not to be served but to*
> *serve, and to give his life as a ransom for many."*
> Matthew 20:28

It's no secret that most people who attend church services come as consumers rather than servants. We see the foolishness in this, but it feels as if we have resigned ourselves to it. We have learned to accept it as though there's nothing we can do about it. People put money in the offering basket, which pays for the staff salaries, so the staff should do their jobs and minister to the people. It sounds like a fair and efficient system, and it works pretty well in some places. It's not what God wanted, but it works.

> *"So if there is any encouragement in Christ, any comfort*
> *from love, any participation in the Spirit, any affection*
> *and sympathy, complete my joy by being of the same mind,*
> *having the same love, being in full accord and of one*
> *mind. Do nothing from selfish ambition or conceit, but in*
> *humility count others more significant than yourselves. Let*
> *each of you look not only to his own interests, but also to*

the interests of others. Have this mind among yourselves,
which is yours in Christ Jesus, who, though he was in the
form of God, did not count equality with God a thing
to be grasped, but emptied himself, by taking the form of
a servant, being born in the likeness of men. And being
found in human form, he humbled himself by becoming
obedient to the point of death, even death on a cross."

Philippians 2:1–8

God wants you to resemble His Son, especially when you gather with your church family. Do you show up to gatherings looking to serve? As some of you read that question, you feel burdened—like a weight was just placed on you. You already live a busy life, and you want the church gathering to be a place of rest, where you can be fed. If you think that sitting back and letting the church staff feed you will bring you the most fulfillment, you are so wrong. God promised that those who give will be most blessed (Acts 20:35). Takers are the most miserable people on earth. It is our inability to take our eyes off ourselves and put them onto others that destroys us. This is what Jesus saves us from. This is what the Holy Spirit wants to do in us. The most humble people are typically the happiest.

Imagine gathering with a group of people who were trying to outserve one another. Have you ever been in a room filled with humble people who count others more significant than themselves? It's anything but burdensome. When servants gather together, everyone is built up. No one hates consumerism more than God, because that mentality keeps the church from having the vibrancy He intended. Don't give up on the dream. The church doesn't have to remain a group of needy people complaining that they haven't been fed well enough. It really can become a group of servants who thrive in serving.

EXPERIENCING GOD

Paul explained to the church in Corinth that every person in their congregation was given a supernatural ability to bless others in the church. He even called these abilities "manifestation[s] of the Spirit" (1 Cor. 12:7; 14:12). Does that image stir any excitement in you? To see God Himself move through a human body! Some of us have seen demons possess bodies and speak through them; others have seen Hollywood depictions of this. We read of it in Scripture. We can imagine a demon having complete control of someone, to make him or her speak and move according to its pleasure.

Why is it that most of us have a clearer picture of demon possession than manifestations of the Holy Spirit? Most of us would say we believe in demon possession, but do we really believe the Spirit could work through us to an even greater extent? Our gatherings were meant to look otherworldly! We would be terrified for days if we saw a demon-possessed woman, so shouldn't a Spirit-filled woman be equally startling and memorable? We need to expect more! Wouldn't you be thrilled about the next church gathering if you knew that the Holy Spirit was going to literally manifest through someone? Everyone?

We have become too easily satisfied. We are content if a person leaves pleased. God wants them awed. I'm not suggesting that we try to make our services bizarre by bringing in deadly snakes. Nor am I saying that we try to hype ourselves into some sort of emotional frenzy that lacks any God-birthed substance. I am saying that we have settled for the natural and our choices give little evidence that we believe in the Holy Spirit. For that reason, we end up with gatherings that are very explainable and at times feel mechanical and even obligatory.

Paul wanted all believers showing up with a confidence that God wanted to move through them, possessing them and manifesting Himself through them to build up those who gathered. Do you approach gatherings with that expectation? If you are content to receive from others, you will miss out on the thrill of having the Spirit manifest Himself through you. This will cause you to be dissatisfied and the Church to suffer. Your gift is needed.

Traditionally, the Church values people the same way the world does. We look for great leaders, strong communicators, and talented artists. We value their gifts and put them on display. Just like the world, we overlook so many who don't initially appear to have much to offer. Do our actions show that we expect supernatural contributions from every member of the body? We would never dream of looking God in the face and telling Him we thought one of His children was worthless. But we don't have to say it with our lips if our actions scream it.

My fellow elders and I repented after studying 1 Corinthians 12–14 a couple of years ago. We realized that there were many in our congregation we didn't expect much of. We began praying for them by name and approaching them individually to encourage them. We decided to find the most overlooked in our congregation to remind them of biblical truth and tell them how badly we needed them. After all, in the context of 1 Corinthians, didn't Paul explain that it was through the overlooked that God chose to display His power (1:26–27)? How would we act if we believed that? Are we not overvaluing the rich, beautiful, and talented just as the world does? So many people often slip in and out of services without much notice. For some reason, the millionaires, CEOs, and famous are always noticed. Does that tell us anything?

THE TASK OF GIFTED LEADERS

We have to stop viewing church leaders as people who minister to us. God clearly explained their role. It was not to coddle

you but to equip you. Think personal trainer, not massage
therapist. *You are someones personal trainer*

> *"And he gave the apostles, the prophets, the evangelists,*
> *the shepherds and teachers, to equip the saints for the*
> *work of ministry, for building up the body of Christ."*
> Ephesians 4:11–12

Our Father thinks all His children are extremely gifted.
God is convinced He did an amazing job in creating each of
them and supernaturally empowering them. His desire is to
see all His kids serve to their full potential. He placed church
leaders on the earth to ensure this would happen. Few people
understand this to be the role of their church leaders, and the
leaders themselves often don't understand their role. Leaders
have become like personal trainers who lift the weights for
their clients. They run on the treadmill while their trainees
sit and marvel. Then we wonder why we the people aren't
developing.

There is a wall in our house with a ton of marks on it.
It's where my kids measure themselves every few months to
see whether they have grown. They get so excited with every
quarter inch (Lisa and I produce short kids), and there's a look
of disappointment when they've stayed the same height for too
long. They want to see growth! Most new parents are measur-
ing and weighing their newborns to make sure they are being

fed enough. If the baby isn't growing, they panic and make serious changes. Growth is expected.

Why isn't this expected in the Church? Week after week, the same faces show up with little to no change in their lives. Insanely, we just keep doing the same thing, hoping it will yield different results. Every week, same small talk, same "Good sermon," same "See you next week." If there's no fruit, isn't it time for change? I recently heard someone say, "Your organization is perfectly designed for producing the results you're experiencing right now." It may be time for a serious shift.

Even if we wanted all people to use their gifts, is it even possible with the way we currently do things? There isn't time. When we reduce "church" to a ninety-minute service where one person teaches for forty-five minutes and another leads music for thirty minutes, we are left with fifteen minutes for announcements and forced handshakes with the people sitting near you. Are we creating the space necessary for every person to feel like he or she can be used by God to encourage and build up others? Have we made our churches so professional and impressive that only the polished few can contribute?

In speaking of the church, Paul said, "When each part is working properly, makes the body grow so that it builds itself up in love" (Eph. 4:16). A church grows to maturity only when each part is "working." If we give up on the goal of having all members exercise their spiritual gifts, we are destined for perpetual immaturity.

WHAT ARE WE PRODUCING?

If everyone who graduated from Harvard ended up working at a Jack in the Box, who in their right mind would spend the fortune required to send their kids there? Harvard is supposed to produce professionals ready to compete for high-level positions. In the same way, Paul expected the Church to produce courageous, hardworking saints, who are unfazed by false teachings and able to resist temptation (Eph. 4:11–14). In describing his goal for those he pastored, Paul used the phrases "mature manhood" and "the measure of the stature of the fullness of Christ" (v. 13). Does this describe your church members?

We have high expectations from spending four years at Harvard. We should expect even greater results from four years (or four decades!) in the Church.

At the end of the day, it's about what we produce. We can get so focused on getting people through our doors that we don't think about what goes out. The Church's purpose is not just to exist. It's to produce. Are we producing mature disciples who imitate Christ by constantly serving others? Are we developing communities that are so deeply in love with one another that the world marvels (John 13:34–35)? If this is not being produced, why do we exist?

I echo what Mike Breen wrote: "Are we just good at getting people together once a week and maybe into a small group, or are we actually good at producing the types of people we read about in the New Testament? Have we shifted our criteria for a good disciple as someone who shows up to our stuff, gives money and occasionally feeds poor people?"[1]

BECOMING ATTRACTIVE

Twenty years ago, my wife went to the gym (it's not her thing). When she got home, I asked her how it went. She proceeded to tell me she took a step class (a big deal in the 1990s), but she didn't get much out of the workout. When I asked her why, she explained that the instructor was so obese that it was hard to be motivated by her. Lisa wasn't trying to be mean. She was just used to having an instructor who makes her envious. This is how they sell fitness machines on television because they know it motivates us. They find a totally chiseled man or woman working out on one of their machines and tempt you to pull out your credit card in hope of becoming like them.

When I read about the apostle Paul, I am challenged to become like him. When I read of his longing for Christ (Phil. 1:21–26), perseverance through suffering (2 Cor. 11:16–33), and love for people (Rom. 9:1–3), it stirs me. I want to look like him. I want his peace. Like Paul, I want to come to the end of my life and know that I didn't waste it. It's his example, not his words, that moves me.

Even though there are well-known talk-show hosts, bloggers, and speakers, nobody really admires them. They just talk. Speakers can fool some, but everyone admires the life that's worthy of following. It seems we have lost some of this reality in the Church. We expect people to be captivated by our speech when our lifestyles are not that compelling. We pat ourselves on the back when we can showcase some happy families with virgin children who don't swear.

That is hardly proof God is with us and not with them. If we were able to look objectively, we could see why the average person is not banging on the front doors of our church buildings.

If Muslims were advertising free doughnuts and a raffle for a free iPad as a means to get people to their events, I would find that ridiculous. It would be proof to me that their god does not answer prayer. If they needed rock concerts and funny speakers to draw crowds, I would see them as desperate and their god as cheap and weak. Understand that I am not judging any church that works hard at getting people through the doors with good motives. I spent years doing the same thing, and I believe my heart was sincere. I wanted people to hear the gospel by any means possible. Praise God for people who have a heart for truth! I'm just asking you to consider how this looks to a watching world. While our good intentions may have gotten some people in the door, they also may have caused a whole generation to have a lower view of our God.

It is hard for the average person to reconcile why a group of people supposedly filled with God's Spirit, able to speak with the Creator of the universe, would need gimmicks.

NO LONGER CHURCH

Is there ever a point when a church is no longer a church? Is it only when the doctrinal statement no longer declares that Jesus is the Son of God? Just because you walk into a building with the word *Church* painted on a sign doesn't mean God sees it as an actual church.

Suppose I was concerned about people's health so I opened Chan's Healthy Juice Stop. I rented a building and painted a cool sign with a bunch of happy vegetables on it. I began making drinks by blending kale, carrots, beets, and spinach. My customers loved my drinks and came daily. There was just one problem: there aren't enough health fanatics to keep my business afloat. My solution: whipped cream. Once I topped my drinks with it, more people started coming around. Soon after, I added chocolate syrup and sales grew even more. Once gummy bears and M&M's were introduced, I started making a fortune. I would still boast that my drinks contained some healthy ingredients, even though I knew my clients were getting fatter and more lethargic. My desire to run a lucrative business at some point overpowered my original goal of health. At some point in the process, I should have taken down the sign.

This is a common scenario in churches. Prayer, Communion, fellowship, and Bible reading don't attract large crowds. So we start adding elements that will attract people. We accomplish a goal, but it is the wrong goal. There comes a point when so many additions are made that you can no longer call it a church.— *Some do it w/ additions Better than others*

I agree with the poignant words of A. W. Tozer when he wrote, "Our most pressing obligation today is to do all in our power to obtain a revival that will result in a reformed, revitalized, purified church. It is of far greater importance that we have better Christians than that we have more of them."[2]

FORCING THE ISSUE

Don't you see the weirdness in calling people CHRISTian when they aren't servants? I know we can't force people to serve, but there has to be something we can do. No team puts up with players who refuse to contribute. No army puts up with soldiers who don't carry their own weight. Why do churches continue to put up with Christians who refuse to *Do we give them opportunity* serve? Why don't we treat selfishness as a sin that needs to be confronted? If Scripture commands us to serve one another, isn't it a bit strange that we give people a free pass?

*"As each has received a gift, use it to serve one
another, as good stewards of God's varied grace."*
1 Peter 4:10

*"So whoever knows the right thing to do
and fails to do it, for him it is sin."*
James 4:17

We confront sexual immorality in our churches because
we are commanded to live holy lives. The adulterous person
does not represent Christ well. But neither does the consumer.
It's a sin that has to be confronted if we want to give the world
an accurate representation of the body of Christ. And if we
really loved our brothers and sisters, shouldn't we be encouraging them to repent?

As pastors, we began having talks with people in our congregation who didn't serve. Not only was it selfish, hurting
the body, keeping them from manifesting the Spirit, but it
was clearly sinful. It was out of a deep love for them that we
wanted to see them have victory in this area. Sometimes a little
pressure is good.

Two of my closest friends are Al and Christian. Both
of them are men who know how to persevere. Al can be
exhausted and still run another three miles. Christian can be
stuffed and still eat another three tacos. A couple years ago,
when I wanted to get in shape, guess who I called. (Yes, I have

permission from Christian to write this. In fact, he asked me to let people know that his life verse is Leviticus 3:16.) I asked Al to push me and do whatever he needed to do to get me in shape. There were many days when Al annoyed me with his constant pressure, yelling at me to run faster or lift more than I wanted. While sweating like a pig, on the verge of passing out, I would have visions of sitting at a Chinese buffet with Christian. Meanwhile, Al just kept talking, refusing to let me quit. It has been miserable, but I'm in the best shape of my life now. Pressure can be a great thing.

I remember the day Lisa and I brought our firstborn home from the hospital. Neither of us knew what we were doing, but we were forced to figure it out. We had no choice. We loved our baby, so we refused to be lousy parents. Seven kids later, I think we're getting pretty good at this.

Ministry really isn't that different. No one is truly ready for a life of shepherding others, but we step up to the challenge when we are thrown into the position. Sometimes the most loving thing we can do is challenge those we love, and a little pressure doesn't hurt. I remember being a senior in high school when my youth pastor asked me to lead a dozen freshman guys. I had never discipled anyone before, but I was eager to serve God however He wanted. After a few weeks, God gave me a real love for these guys and a deep concern for their walk with God. I was far from a perfect leader, but I did my best. I don't know where I would be today if I wasn't challenged to serve and pushed to lead at an early age. I would have missed out on a very full and blessed life.

We currently have around forty pastors who lead our churches in San Francisco. They all work other jobs. None of them are paid by the church. They never received formal training to become pastors. It has all been on-the-job training from the elders. They have grown because they have felt the pressure of pastoral responsibility. They have become great pastors and are making disciples who will soon be pastors also. I love these men, and I trust them with my life. I trust them with my children.

I could tell you stories of people who have sacrificed rooms in their homes, cars, money, privacy, health, and vacations in order to serve others. I could speak of miracles, healings, and prophecies coming from the most unlikely people. These results have come from expecting every member to serve. To me, however, the greatest blessing has been watching the leaders develop.

The Church was supposed to be a breeding ground for pastors and elders. Every church should be equipping people and sending them out. Unfortunately, the trend is the opposite. We send out want ads, asking for pastors to come serve at our churches. Some churches even hire professional headhunters to find pastors for them. Rather than sending, we are recruiting. This has become normal.

We can develop leaders only when we structure things in a way that requires others to lead. I had to learn how to limit the use of my gifts in order to make space for others to lead. The result has been an army of equipped leaders who could be dropped off in any city in the world and they would be capable of making a living while making disciples. They have shown themselves capable of starting and multiplying churches. They are servant leaders raising up more servant leaders to be sent out.

It's time to put some loving pressure on ourselves and those around us. This is everyone's responsibility. Only when we become servants will we experience the Holy Spirit as Jesus intended. Only then will the Church resemble the Christ they worship.

Only then will the Church resemble the Christ they Worship.

6

GOOD SHEPHERDS

Of all the chapters in this book, this is the one that was written with the most prayer and love. It is the most heartfelt and the one chapter that brought me to tears. I have been a pastor for over thirty years. It is all I have ever known. I knew of my calling when I was a kid, and I am sure of it to this day. Even when I have tried to run from the responsibility, God kept bringing me back. I love being a pastor. I love helping people understand God and fall in love with Him. Even with the betrayals and heartbreaks, I can't think of anything I would rather do. If my life was to end today (and it might), I can't express how full my life has been. I count it an honor to be called to ministry, and I shake my head in wonder that He chose me to do this. Few people get to do what they love so much.

I write this chapter to full-time pastors, to bivocational pastors, and to many of you reading this, who, unbeknownst to you, will be called to shepherd others. I believe that thousands of you are called to pastor, not according to the traditional understanding of that role but in a biblical sense. I write this in hope that you will love this calling even more than I have. I also write with eternity in mind. Not all of you will hear "Well done" from the mouth of God, but I want you to. Meanwhile, the Enemy is constantly trying to lure us all away from our first love and make us people pleasers. Paul gave loving warnings to young Timothy at the end of his life, and I have tried to write this with a similar heart. I understand many of the pitfalls because I have stumbled into them myself.

As I mentioned in the start of this book, I tried to pay special attention to the times when God used the strongest language in the biblical narrative. In my opinion, God spoke more severely to leaders than to any other group. On the one hand, God's most tender and honoring speech was reserved for spiritual leaders. It seems as if He had unique relationships with leaders and He was even defensive of them. For example, He struck Miriam with leprosy when she dared speak against Moses (Num. 12:1–10), and He caused a couple of bears to maul forty-two people when they mocked Elisha (2 Kings

2:23–24). John was called "beloved" (John 21:20–24), and Abraham was "a friend of God" (James 2:23).

On the other hand, some of God's most condemning words were also spoken to leaders. The pursuit of leadership comes with severe warnings. James said leaders will be judged more harshly (3:1), and the writer of Hebrews said leaders will give an account for how they shepherd (13:17). Jesus addressed the religious leaders of His day as children of hell (Matt. 23:15). The point is that we should not assume anyone in a position of spiritual authority deserves to be there.

This was a difficult chapter to write because I want to be careful of arrogance and disrespect, but I have to do something with the examples of Christ, Peter, and Paul—all of whom strongly rebuked false teaching. Somehow we need to follow David's example of being careful and respectful toward even terrible leaders while also following Paul's example in calling out false teachers.

As I look over my life, I believe I have been overly critical and disrespectful at times while being cowardly and too political at other times. I don't have all the answers here, nor do I believe I've been exemplary. God has been patient in teaching me how to say difficult things with a spirit of love rather than judgment. And He constantly reminds me that I need to examine myself first. That is where we all need to start.

For those in church leadership, we can't assume we belong there. We have to ask ourselves, *Am I sure I should be in this position? Am I in a good place to lead? Is my relationship with Jesus one that I want replicated?*

For those not currently leading others, don't assume you shouldn't. It could be that your fear of failure is keeping you from doing what God created and called you to do. No one is called to be constantly fed without leading and feeding others. Turn around and look. If there is no one following you, something is wrong with your life. God has called you to the work of making disciples. He has called you to lead in some capacity.

This is not a chapter for laypersons to use in judgment of their leaders. The challenge of leading this generation of highly opinionated individuals is daunting enough. I definitely don't want to add fuel to that fire. This chapter is written for all of us, to make us evaluate our own lives. The Church needs godly leaders. Contrary to popular belief, we are all called to pastor (a word that simply means "shepherd"). Older women are to shepherd the younger (Titus 2:3–5). Parents are to shepherd their children (Eph. 6:4). Timothy was told to teach others what he himself had been taught (2 Tim. 2:2). We're all called to be making disciples (Matt. 28:19–20). If you can't find a single person who looks to you as a mentor, something is wrong with you. And social media doesn't count. I'm talking about flesh-and-blood humans who mimic your actions. This requires living a life that's worth duplicating, which is quite a bit harder than posting pictures and quotes.

THE TRAPS OF MINISTRY

Some of the expectations we place on leaders make their success nearly impossible. They are no longer prioritizing the things God wants them to prioritize or the things they hoped to do when they first began ministering to others, and that's not entirely their fault. Many entered ministry because of a deep love for God and people. They had a fearless and radical mind-set, ready to risk everything for the Kingdom. But there are so many traps laid out for ministers today. Eventually they fall into one of them and become distracted, deceived, or depressed.

The Trap of Avoiding Criticism. People say harsh things to pastors. No matter what is preached, there are people on both sides anxious to criticize. The harshness or sheer amount of criticism often causes a politicizing of the pulpit. They sound less like prophets and more like they are running for office. The leader becomes overly aware of how people respond and starts teaching in a way that avoids criticism rather than fearlessly preaching truth.

The Trap of Fund-Raising. I don't know of any pastors who went into ministry because of their love of raising funds. And I don't know of many pastors who are not regularly worried about the church budget or building projects.

The Trap of Comparison. Church members regularly listen to podcasts of gifted speakers, read articles by brilliant theologians, and watch videos of talented church leaders moving thousands of people. It's hard for both leaders and followers not to become discouraged by the comparisons.

The Trap of Meeting Expectations. People come on Sunday mornings expecting coffee, good parking, music they enjoy at a preferred volume, a thirty-minute sermon, a good nursery, children's ministry, something for preteens, middle school ministry, high school ministry, college/singles' ministry, etc. They are too busy creating what people expect to actually pursue what God commands.

The Trap of Popularity. Empty seats are a downer, and watching people flood to the church down the street can be depressing. Then try going to a Christian conference and seeing celebrity pastors treated like royalty. It's hard not to become envious and hard for those who have "made it" not to become proud. This system has no winners.

The Trap of Safety. We place our pastors in a church office surrounded by Christians for forty hours a week and then ask them to teach us about living by faith.

The Trap of Greed. People in our country feel more entitled than ever, and pastors are no exception. The larger the church, the larger the paycheck. The higher the book sales, the higher the royalties. For those who like to live comfortably, church growth can have mixed motives.

The Trap of Demonic Attack. On top of it all, there is a roaring lion seeking to devour (1 Pet. 5:8), and pastors are on the top of the list. There is an Enemy doing everything he can to tempt you into sinning in a way that harms the reputation of the Church.

You can argue that pastors should be strong enough to avoid these traps, or you can argue that people should stop setting so many traps. Regardless of whose fault it is, it is clear that leaders are distracted and discouraged. Can we really expect Spirit-filled disciples to be produced from that kind of leadership? Are we unknowingly setting up godly men and women for failure?

THE TIMES HAVE CHANGED

When I started Cornerstone Church back in 1994, things were much different than they are now. People were more respectful toward pastors and authority in general. There was no such thing as social media. Few people even had cell phones! (Yes, I'm ancient.) If someone wanted to encourage or criticize me, they would have to find me. Times have changed.

I remember when social media started to flood the world. Suddenly it became easier and easier for anyone to flatter or criticize me publicly. There were days when my head could barely fit through the door because of all the compliments. There were other times when I battled hurt and anger over harsh statements that were made. I have learned over time to pay less attention to these things, but it was overwhelming at the outset.

For those who have never had to deal with floods of people strongly stating their opinions about you, be grateful. I have met very few people who have navigated that world and remained humble and loving yet courageous. Large crowds do something strange to all of us. We can subconsciously begin preaching to avoid criticism rather than teaching truth regardless of the response. We live in a time when people are so volatile. If we say one wrong word in public, it can wreak havoc.

It is only going to get more difficult for pastors to speak in front of large crowds with boldness and humility. Maybe that's why we are finding fewer pastors known for being humble and courageous. I was deeply affected by a pastor in China who said to me, "In America, pastors think they have to become famous to have a big impact. In China, the most influential Christian leaders had to be the most hidden." My soul leaped when I heard that, imagining a chance to fight for impact and obscurity all at once. It feels as if our current way of doing things in America sets us up for failure. Those who pursue massive Kingdom impact seem to always be fighting a losing battle with pride. It is how the Enemy lures us away from the very character that makes us effective.

> *"Remember your leaders, those who spoke to*
> *you the word of God. Consider the outcome of*
> *their way of life, and imitate their faith."*
>
> Hebrews 13:7

Leaders, I want to challenge you to examine your lives and see whether you can truly tell people in good conscience to follow you as you follow Christ. For those not yet in positions of leadership, as we go through the qualities that are essential for good, biblical leadership, I urge you to examine your leaders in a spirit of grace and humility to discern whether their faith and way of life is something you want to imitate. For some of you, God may be calling you to step into leadership, and I implore you to devote yourself to growing in the following areas.

THE CHRISTIAN PASTOR

That heading may sound ridiculous, but is it really safe to assume all pastors are Christians? Just because we claim to believe in Him or went to school to study for ministry, it doesn't ensure that our hearts are His. Having spent two years in a Bible college and three years in seminary, I can tell you that a degree can be proof of intelligence or discipline but not spirituality. Those were easily the five worst years of my life. Remember that in Jesus' day, some of the religious leaders were the most evil. Scripture is always warning us to be on guard against false teachers.

"But false prophets also arose among the people,
just as there will be false teachers among you, who

will secretly bring in destructive heresies, even
denying the Master who bought them, bringing
upon themselves swift destruction. And many will
follow their sensuality, and because of them the
way of truth will be blasphemed. And in their
greed they will exploit you with false words."

2 Peter 2:1–3

There will always be false teachers on this earth. Jesus taught that wolves will come in sheep's clothing (Matt. 7:15). What better camouflage than as a minister? Some will teach false doctrine because of their desire to be accepted. Others will preach truth while living a lie. Whether it's their message or lifestyle that is false, both are condemned. If you read the rest of 2 Peter 2, you will see that terrifying judgment is reserved for them. If you are reading this and are living an immoral life, it's time to step down. The worst thing you can be is a false teacher. There is nothing more evil you can do during your few years on earth than to lead people away from their Creator.

I have prayed that everyone who reads this section will actually take time to evaluate his or her own life. As Paul said, "Examine yourselves, to see whether you are in the faith" (2 Cor. 13:5). Is it clear that you have counted the cost and decided to follow Jesus? Do your pastors show clear evidence that they have forsaken all to follow Him?

THE PRAYING PASTOR

I once told my staff to let me know if they were not praying at least an hour a day. This way I could replace them with someone who would. I would much rather hire someone who prayed and did nothing else than someone who worked tirelessly without praying. That may sound harsh, but prayer is that critical. Prayer is not merely a task of ministry; it is a gauge that exposes our hearts' condition. It unveils our pride, showing us whether or not we believe we are powerless apart from God. When we pray, it is an expression of surrender to God and reliance on His infinite wisdom and sovereignty. Even Jesus Himself would not take matters into His own hands when His disciple Peter was being attacked by Satan.

> *"Simon, Simon, behold, Satan demanded*
> *to have you, that he might sift you like*
> *wheat, but I have prayed for you that your*
> *faith may not fail. And when you have*
> *turned again, strengthen your brothers."*
> Luke 22:31–32

If anyone should have been able to help Peter with good counseling or teaching, it would have been almighty Jesus. Yet His solution was to pray. Meditate on that for a moment.

Prayer is the mark of a lover. Those who deeply love Jesus can't help but pray often. To love God with our entire being is the greatest command in Scripture. Pastors who are not drawn to prayer should not be pastors. It is in prayer that we seek the Lord and the welfare of our people.

I have been joining with my elders to pray Ephesians 3:14–19 over our people, begging God that they would long for Jesus as we do.

A pastor from India once told me he was researching movements and noticed a common thread: movements of God always start with a leader who knows God deeply, and they always end when the followers know only the leader deeply. Pastors, we must know Him deeply and make disciples whose primary attachment is to Christ Himself.

THE HUMBLE PASTOR

Another pastor from India gave me some simple and powerful advice I hope never leaves me. His ministry has led over three million people to Jesus. All these people are being discipled. When I asked how he organized this massive army, he replied, "Americans always want to know about strategy. This is what I will tell you: my leaders are the most humble men I know, and they know Jesus deeply." He proceeded to tell me that his biggest mistakes were the times when he allowed people into leadership who were not humble. He got so excited about releasing their gifts, but it always led to their destruction. To this day, he says those are his biggest regrets. Now his main criterion for identifying leaders is humility, and his leadership problems have significantly decreased.

We would never admit it, but we often search for leaders the way the world does. We look at outward appearances. We want a great speaker and gifted leader. God has always championed the humble person who passionately seeks Him. It seems that many pastors may have started as humble prayer warriors but let the expectations of people sway their priorities. Others have made little pretense of humility but have only been encouraged to advance in ministry due to their charisma.

> *"Or do you suppose it is to no purpose that the Scripture says, 'He yearns jealously over the spirit that he has made to dwell in us'? But he gives more grace. Therefore it says, 'God opposes the proud but gives grace to the humble.' Submit yourselves therefore to God. Resist the devil, and he will flee from you. Draw near to God, and he will draw near to you. Cleanse your hands, you sinners, and purify your hearts, you double-minded. Be wretched and mourn and weep. Let your laughter be turned to mourning and your joy to gloom. Humble yourselves before the Lord, and he will exalt you."*
>
> James 4:5–10

Nothing can be worse than the opposition of God. James made it clear: "God opposes the proud" person (v. 6). How effective can a church be if God is opposed to its leader? On the contrary, God promised to draw near and show grace to the humble person who draws near to Him.

One of the questions I often ask myself before I preach is, Will this sermon draw attention to Christ or to me? For many of us, our default is self-preservation and self-exaltation. In our insecurity, we worry about what people will think of us rather than hoping they will not. I have struggled with this my whole life. It's ugly.

In speaking of humankind, Jesus said there was "no one greater" than John the Baptist (Matt. 11:11). He was great in God's eyes because he didn't seek to be great in people's eyes. John said of Jesus, "He must increase, but I must decrease" (John 3:30).

THE LOVING PASTOR

Once again, this doesn't seem like it's worth mentioning. Why else would a person become a pastor? Is there such a thing as a pastor who doesn't genuinely love people?

It has been my experience that it is very easy to "do ministry" without loving people. Love is not necessary to be a "successful" pastor in our country. I can think of many seasons in my life when I was busy ministering to people with no real feelings of love toward them. It is very easy to see people as projects that you want to fix rather than children you deeply love.

I love Paul's example! Read this carefully:

> *"For we never came with words of flattery, as you know, nor with a pretext for greed—God is witness. Nor did we seek glory from people, whether from you or from others, though we could have made demands as apostles of Christ. But we were gentle among you, like a nursing mother taking care of her own children. So, being affectionately desirous of you, we were ready to share with you not only the gospel of God but also our own selves, because you had become very dear to us. For you remember, brothers, our labor and toil: we worked night and day, that we might not be a burden to any of you, while we proclaimed to you the gospel of God. You are witnesses, and God also, how holy and righteous and blameless was our conduct toward you believers. For you know how, like a father with his children, we exhorted each one of you and encouraged you and charged you to walk in a manner worthy of God, who calls you into his own kingdom and glory."*
>
> 1 Thessalonians 2:5–12

When Paul spoke about his time with this church, he said he was "like a nursing mother taking care of her own children" (v. 7). Imagine how amazing it would be to have a pastor care for you in this way! Paul went on to say that he also exhorted them "like a father with his children" (v. 11). He showed not only the tender care of a nursing mother but also the exhortation of a strong father. Too many pastors are aspiring to be great writers, speakers, and leaders. There are not enough who are known as great moms and dads. And those who serve well as moms and dads never become known because this isn't highly valued. You won't be celebrated on a large scale for humbly caring for a group of people.

If one of our primary goals in the Church is the perfect unity Jesus prayed for in John 17, then it has to start with leaders who love their people. We are to be parents, not babysitters. There is a huge difference. Most know that having children is a huge commitment. It takes away your freedom, privacy, and time. But it is so worth it.

THE EQUIPPING PASTOR

Part of my responsibility as a good dad is to make sure I raise my kids in such a way that they are capable of leaving my home to start their own. I have a few short years to prepare them for the world out there. My job is to train them to stand on their own rather than be dependent on me. This should be the goal of every pastor as well. If we are not careful, we end up with people who have been sitting in churches for years and complaining they aren't being fed to their liking. This is the same kind of dysfunction as a thirty-year-old complaining about his mom's cooking. The goal of a good pastor is to raise up good pastors.

> *"And he gave the apostles, the prophets, the evangelists,*
> *the shepherds and teachers, to equip the saints for the*
> *work of ministry, for building up the body of Christ,*
> *until we all attain to the unity of the faith and of the*
> *knowledge of the Son of God, to mature manhood, to*
> *the measure of the stature of the fullness of Christ, so*
> *that we may no longer be children, tossed to and fro by*
> *the waves and carried about by every wind of doctrine,*
> *by human cunning, by craftiness in deceitful schemes."*
>
> Ephesians 4:11–14

One of the most debilitating issues facing the Church is the lack of maturing her members. Churches are filled with children who never grow up to become parents. And they're not expected to. Many pastors expect their members to sit under their teachings till they die rather than training them to leave and shepherd others. Paul was clear that church leaders are to equip the saints for work. Hugh Halter sees this as a trap we build for ourselves: "Many vocational ministers are stuck doing the work of ministry because they take a paycheck from consumer Christians who fail to see the full scope of their calling."[1]

What would happen to our society if parents didn't expect their children to start their own families? This is exactly what has happened in the Church. We have such low expectations for people who are supposedly filled with the Holy Spirit. It is time for spiritual parents (i.e., pastors) to believe in their children again. To stop doing all their chores for them but instead to train them for a lifetime of work. There will always be those who rebel against this, and that's why Paul told Timothy to focus on the "faithful" ones who will go teach others (2 Tim. 2:2).

My goal in shepherding has changed so much. Long gone are the days when I am content with a bunch of people who sing loud, don't divorce, and give to missions. I now want to know I can drop off any member of my church in a city and that person could grow in Jesus, make disciples, and start a church. My faith in the Holy Spirit's power convinces me this is possible. It is in our very DNA. We all have been given a spirit of courage and the power to do beyond what we can imagine. We must train our people to be independently dependent on the Holy Spirit

While many pastors boast of how many children sit under their care, doesn't it make more sense to boast of how many have graduated from their care? Isn't it more a sign of failure when children are unable to leave the house? Raising thousands of consumers is not success.

THE SPIRIT-FILLED PASTOR

When you hear the word *Spirit-filled*, what do you picture? Who do you picture?

I said earlier that we all have a concept of what it looks like for a person to be possessed by a demon but less so by the Holy Spirit. Let me put it this way: we all know that there's a massive difference between a demon-possessed person and one who isn't. Shouldn't there also be a huge difference between the Spirit-filled person and the nice person who doesn't know Jesus? Let's not confuse theological knowledge or general kindness with being Spirit-filled. Is your pastor Spirit-filled? Are you?

Disregard how you imagine a Spirit-filled person acting. Ephesians 5 describes the Spirit-filled person this way:

> *"And do not get drunk with wine, for that is debauchery, but be filled with the Spirit, addressing one another in psalms and hymns and spiritual songs, singing and making melody to the Lord with your heart, giving thanks always and for everything to God the Father in the name of our Lord Jesus Christ, submitting to one another out of reverence for Christ."*
>
> Ephesians 5:18–21

Paul compared it to being drunk. We can all picture a drunk person—the way their speech and movements are impaired. When your body is filled with alcohol, it affects everything. In the same way, when we are filled with the Spirit, we can't do anything without His influence. We open our mouths and God comes out because we are filled with Him. That's why Spirit-filled people are "addressing one another in psalms and hymns and spiritual songs" (v. 19). They are filled with praises for God, so when they talk to you, those praises come out. Spirit-filled people are singing and making melodies in their hearts because that is what the Spirit always wants to do. They are "giving thanks always" (v. 20) because the blessing of the Spirit's presence makes them grateful. They submit to "one another out of reverence for Christ" (v. 21) because they are humble and respect the leadership God has appointed. The Spirit of God affects all their relationships.

Galatians 5:22–23 lists the fruit of the Holy Spirit; most of us are familiar with these. It is easy to look at this list and think, *Yeah, I'm pretty loving, patient, kind, etc. I guess I'm displaying the fruit of the Spirit.* But if our love is a result of the Holy Spirit's work, shouldn't it be outstanding? Overwhelmingly different? Let's not be too hasty in attributing to the Spirit something that others can muster up in the flesh.

Don't we all desire to be led by a pastor who is truly filled with the Spirit? A person who has a supernatural power, boldness, and character? I have been praying for the miraculous.

I am telling the Lord I don't want to just be kind. I want the kindness only the Holy Spirit can produce. How else can we attract the world? I want the peace that surpasses comprehension. A peace that leaves people confused. If pastors don't exemplify these qualities to supernatural proportions, what hope do our churches have?

THE MISSIONAL PASTOR

Jesus commanded us to reach the ends of the earth. This is for His glory, their salvation, and our well-being. We were created for a purpose. We find fulfillment when we stay focused on the mission. Pastors must set the pace in having an urgency for helping those who suffer. We must stay aware of the billions who have never heard the gospel even once. We can't just focus on more creative ways to deliver the gospel to those who have already rejected it a dozen times.

> *"Religion that is pure and undefiled before God the Father is this: to visit orphans and widows in their affliction, and to keep oneself unstained from the world."*
> James 1:27

It is God's heart to be a Father to the fatherless (Ps. 68:5). Those who have His Spirit in them should naturally have compassion for those who suffer. Pastors can fixate on really strange peripheral things when they lose sight of mothers who are watching their children starve to death. We can complain when we forget we have brothers and sisters being cruelly tortured in prisons right now. We have a tendency to argue and divide over trivial matters when we forget hell exists.

Every pastor has given a message on the Great Commission (Matt. 28:16–20). How many are living exemplary lives showing they are serious about Jesus' great command? Let's pray for and become a generation of leaders whose hearts break for the lost and suffering. It's no secret that church buildings are currently full of self-centered people coming to consume. The answer is not just telling them to stop being so selfish. Pastors need to engage them in helping the lost and desperate around the world.

THE SUFFERING PASTOR

We will spend a full chapter discussing our need to be suffering servants, so let me just say to leaders specifically that our people often need more than words. They need to see the example of a leader who rejoices amid suffering. Take time to contemplate your words and actions while going through rough times. As your disciples watched and listened, did they witness Christlike forbearance and endurance?

We are too quick to get discouraged and quit because we have not learned to rejoice in suffering. Show me a pastor who rejoices in suffering, and I will show you a pastor who will be in ministry a long time. When pastors who rejoice in suffering make disciples, you end up with an unstoppable church.

UNLIKELY LEADERS

Some of you may have read this chapter and thought, *My pastor doesn't match up.* This may be true, and in some cases it might be best to walk away from your current leader. That is a very serious decision and should be made only after lots of prayer, humility, and biblical reasoning.

But that was not the point of this chapter. My hope was that each person who reads this would seek to rise up and become that godly leader. It may feel overwhelming to picture yourself becoming a suffering, missional, Spirit-filled, equipping, loving, humble, praying, Christian pastor. But let's remember that this is what the Holy Spirit of God longs to do in you. Don't look at this daunting list in the flesh. Apart from the Holy Spirit, this is clearly impossible. For those of us filled with the Spirit of God, this is everything we want to become. Don't fight against what the Holy Spirit may be trying to do in your life.

There have been times in history when shepherds became corrupt. God confronted the shepherds strongly in the Old Testament (Ezek. 34), and Jesus did the same with the religious leaders of His day. His solution was to replace the professionals and train a group of ordinary, uneducated people to change the world. People like you.

God hates it when we underestimate the potential He created us with. He has always valued faith; people take His words literally. Ephesians 3:20 must be a verse we shape our lives around, not just a catchy quote we paint on our walls. The Church is in dire need of a fresh wave of godly leadership. I pray all existing leaders would be renewed or replaced. May God continue to raise up an army of good shepherds who love Him above all else and live to make the Church become everything God designed it to be.

7

CRUCIFIED

*"I have been crucified with Christ. It is no longer I
who live, but Christ who lives in me. And the life
I now live in the flesh I live by faith in the Son of
God, who loved me and gave himself for me."*

Galatians 2:20

In the Ironman Triathlon, participants swim 2.4 miles, bike 112
miles, and run 26.2 miles.[1] If I asked you to watch it with me,
many of you would consider it. If I asked you to compete in
it with me, that number would drop considerably. There are

millions of people in our country who call themselves Christians because they believe the Christian life is about admiring Christ's example, not realizing it is a call to follow it. If they really understood this, the numbers would drop drastically. The New Testament could not be clearer: we are not just to believe in His crucifixion; we are to be crucified with Christ.

If you listened only to the voice of Jesus, read only the words that came out of His mouth, you would have a very clear understanding of what He requires of His followers. If you listened only to modern preachers and writers, you would have a completely different understanding of what it means to follow Jesus. Could there be a more catastrophic problem than this?

There are millions of men and women who have been taught that they can become Christians and it will cost them nothing. And they believe it! There are even some who have the audacity to teach that life will get better once people pray a prayer and ask Jesus into their hearts. Jesus taught the exact opposite!

Read these words of Jesus slowly and carefully. This is *far* more important than any of the following paragraphs I have written. Interpret His words for yourself.

> *"Now great crowds accompanied him, and he turned*
> *and said to them, 'If anyone comes to me and does not*
> *hate his own father and mother and wife and children*
> *and brothers and sisters, yes, and even his own life, he*

cannot be my disciple. Whoever does not bear his own cross and come after me cannot be my disciple. For which of you, desiring to build a tower, does not first sit down and count the cost, whether he has enough to complete it? Otherwise, when he has laid a foundation and is not able to finish, all who see it begin to mock him, saying, "This man began to build and was not able to finish." Or what king, going out to encounter another king in war, will not sit down first and deliberate whether he is able with ten thousand to meet him who comes against him with twenty thousand? And if not, while the other is yet a great way off, he sends a delegation and asks for terms of peace. So therefore, any one of you who does not renounce all that he has cannot be my disciple."

Luke 14:25–33

Forget what you have been told about praying a prayer and asking Jesus to be your personal Savior. Read what Jesus demanded and ask yourself whether you still want to follow Him.

There was no misinterpreting what Christ was calling for. This is why He had so few disciples. The call to follow Jesus was a call to die. The price tag was front and center. Jesus laid it out from the start and told people to count the cost before they got themselves into something they weren't ready to commit to. Nowadays we just want to talk about the good part—the grace and blessings. And of course grace, forgiveness, and mercy are central to the gospel, but at the same time Jesus was very truthful and up-front about the costliness of the gospel, a concept that we completely neglect.

In doing so, we've lost something so central to the essence of what it means to be Christian. Becoming a Christian is a complete and total surrender of your own desires and flesh to the higher purpose of serving God's glory. It means you die to yourself and put on Christ. That is what you're signing up for.

> *"And calling the crowd to him with his disciples, he said to them, 'If anyone would come after me, let him deny himself and take up his cross and follow me. For whoever would save his life will lose it, but whoever loses his life for my sake and the gospel's will save it. For what does it profit a man to gain the whole world and forfeit his soul? For what can a man give in return for his soul?'"*
>
> Mark 8:34–37

According to Jesus, far from having no cost, following Him will cost you everything. Far from promising a better life, He warned of intense suffering.

> *"Then they will deliver you up to tribulation and put you to death, and you will be hated by all nations for my name's sake. And then many will*

*fall away and betray one another and hate one
another. And many false prophets will arise and
lead many astray. And because lawlessness will be
increased, the love of many will grow cold. But
the one who endures to the end will be saved."*

Matthew 24:9–13

Jesus warned that false teachers would come and "lead many astray" (v. 11). This is why it is imperative all of us diligently study the words of Christ. If the above verses sound foreign to you or contrary to what you have been taught, find some new teachers! Run from any teacher who promises wealth and prosperity in this life. The call to follow Christ is the call to joyfully endure suffering in this life for the promise of eternal blessing in the next.

*"Blessed are you when people hate you and when they
exclude you and revile you and spurn your name as
evil, on account of the Son of Man! Rejoice in that
day, and leap for joy, for behold, your reward is great
in heaven; for so their fathers did to the prophets."*

Luke 6:22–23

*"Woe to you, when all people speak well of you,
for so their fathers did to the false prophets."*

Luke 6:26

WHEN SUFFERING BECOMES STRANGE

Suffering is rarely talked about in the American church. I find this ironic because suffering is *all through* the New Testament. I did a sermon one time where I went through every book of the New Testament and started reading verse after verse about suffering to show it's not just in *one* book. It's not just *one* verse. It's *all over the place*. It's one of the clearest doctrines in the New Testament. Over and over it says that as followers of Christ we're going to suffer for Him; we're going to be hated; we're going to be rejected. I preach messages on suffering and people think it's some kind of strange or new teaching, which is crazy given how prominent it is in the Bible. But we just don't talk about it.

The fact that this is such a major theme throughout the New Testament yet such a lost concept within our churches is a huge problem. The more I study the Gospels, the more I am convinced that those of us who live in the United States have a warped view of what it means to be a "Christian." It is for that reason our churches are in the state they are in. A warped view of Christianity can result only in a warped church. But what if we started over? What if we bulldozed what we currently call "church" and started over with actual Christians?

A believer from a house church in Iran (who can't be named for obvious reasons) explained that people who want to join the church have to sign a written statement agreeing to lose their property, be thrown in jail, and be martyred for their faith. Many Christians are arrested in Iran and either executed or imprisoned for years. Fellowship looks a lot different when the church consists of those who have a biblical understanding of Christianity. Interestingly, some research shows that Iran has the fastest-growing evangelical population in the world![2]

When a friend of mine came back from visiting a church in Iraq, I asked him what the biggest difference was between our church and the church in Iraq. He said, "What we call sanctification, they call prerequisite." In other words, we act as though surrender is a lifelong process where we slowly decide whether or not we will give up certain things to God. Meanwhile, the believers in Iraq teach the way Jesus taught. They are required to count the cost, surrendering everything up front; otherwise they cannot join the Church.

Years ago, I was in China and visited an underground church gathering where I asked them about the persecution. And each person who stood up started sharing stories about persecution he or she had endured. Sometimes they had to hide in the walls because the government officials were coming. Some of them had even run from gunshots. But I wish you could hear the way they were sharing. Everyone was just laughing like it was a party! It sounded completely insane to me, hearing them laugh about being shot at. But it didn't faze them, because they just expected it.

And in their prayers, they were screaming out to God to take them to the most dangerous places. "I want to suffer for You. I don't want to go to a safe place. I don't. Please! I want to be counted *worthy* to die in Your name." That's the way they prayed. If you have a group like that, how are you going to stop them? That's the way the Church is supposed to be—an unstoppable force—ready to take a hit and go right back into battle.

I remember later speaking to a man who leads a whole network of churches in China. He told me about how there was a period when there was a little more religious freedom. He decided to test the waters and build a church above ground, just to see how well it would go. His church grew to a couple thousand people. Then the government went in and, sure enough, shut it down and hauled him and the other pastors away. In hindsight, he told me he was actually really grateful because it brought them back to their DNA again. He told me they had started to lose it with the change of structure. By having a large service, people began coming just to listen to a sermon. Once they grew accustomed to merely sitting and listening, he had a hard time stirring the people to action. It was almost as if the Lord used them being torn down again to rebuild even stronger. So they went back.

He explained further that they had started out with five pillars to the house church movement. He began naming the pillars, and at first I was tracking with him. The first one is based on a deep, deep commitment to prayer. The second is commitment to the Word of God. It wasn't about the speaker but about everyone learning the Word of God, reading the Word of God. The third was being committed to the sharing of the gospel, so every member was sharing the gospel. These first three I felt lined up pretty well with what we were trying to do in San Francisco. The fourth was a regular expectation of miracles. Because of their prayer life, because of what they believed of the Holy Spirit, they expected the supernatural. That's something we were growing in desiring and understanding.

But then, with the fifth pillar, he completely blindsided me. He said, "The fifth pillar was we embraced suffering for the glory of Christ." Whoa! He told me this is what they built their church on: *embracing* suffering. It struck me as weird then because I never would have thought of it. But the more I thought about it, the more convinced I became that they were right to include it. It is spoken of all throughout Scripture. They included suffering in the plan for their church, just as the New Testament exhorts us to. And it showed in their fruit! Their church, when they stayed true to their original DNA, produced a group of people who were on fire for Jesus, willing to go wherever and do whatever—no matter the cost.

That's what you read with the early church in Acts 5:40–41: "When they had called in the apostles, they beat them and charged them not to speak in the name of Jesus, and let them go. Then they left the presence of the council, rejoicing that they were counted worthy to suffer dishonor for the name." Think about that for a second: "rejoicing that they were counted worthy to suffer dishonor for the name." How are you going to stop people like that? That was the problem with the government and the early church. They were saying, "How do we stop these guys? We kill them, and they're happier. We torture them, and they walk away rejoicing. We can't stop them. Are we just going to kill them all—just to not listen to them anymore? They're rejoicing in this. They get stronger through persecution."

Until we embrace the suffering that so many Christians embrace around the world, we're not going to have an unstoppable Church. The Enemy is fighting so hard to keep us from reaching that place, because once we get there, he has no foothold.

NOT OF THIS WORLD

Over the past decade, it has been refreshing to see Christians have a greater awareness of people's thoughts and feelings. Rather than quickly judging and labeling people, they take time to listen to their stories and consider their hurts and desires. This is a good thing. In so doing, however, many have made a damning mistake: they have lost sight of God's thoughts and desires. In their compassion for people, they have ignored the holiness of God. They have forgotten that what God feels about an issue dwarfs what any human feels. Or every human.

> *"Let God be true though every one were a liar."*
> Romans 3:4

In an effort to be sensitive to others, we often lose sight of truth. When we do this, we no longer help people but damn them. True compassion takes into account far more than what a person feels today; it takes into account what he or she will feel on judgment day. What some do in the name of being open-minded and compassionate is actually done out of self-love and cowardice. We want to be accepted, so we listen and coddle but refuse to rebuke. If that is love, then the prophets, apostles, and Jesus were the most unloving people to ever walk the planet.

On the contrary, Jesus loved so deeply that He was willing to suffer a lifetime of rejection, even rejection from His Father on the cross. Jesus never lost sight of God's holiness and the offensiveness of sin. He suffered for speaking truth, showing us that true love is often rejected. This was the way of Jesus. This is the way of love.

We may never have to run from physical suffering like our brothers and sisters around the world, but many have chosen to run from the suffering of rejection. More and more often, people are starting to water down their convictions because they don't want to offend anyone. Instead of embracing the persecution that comes with standing out from and against the world, we have begun to embrace the world to try to convince it to tolerate us. That's not the way it was supposed to be.

> *"If the world hates you, know that it has hated me before it hated you. If you were of the world, the world would love you as its own; but because you are not of the world, but I chose you out of the world, therefore the world hates you. Remember the word that I said to you: 'A servant is not greater than his master.' If they persecuted me, they will also persecute you."*
>
> John 15:18–20

When Jesus confronted the Pharisees, He did not mince words, addressing them with "You brood of vipers" (Matt. 3:7; 12:34; 23:33; Luke 3:7) and other such terminology. When He saw people trying to make a profit by money changing and selling sacrifice animals in the temple, He accused them of desecrating the temple of God and flipped over their tables (Matt. 21:12–17; Mark 11:15–19; Luke 19:45–48; John 2:13–22). Jesus felt a righteous anger toward the hypocrisy of the Pharisees and the greed and disrespect of the money changers. Has it ever struck you that besides Jesus no one else seemed to recognize the sin of these two groups of people? You don't see the crowds of Jewish temple-goers confronting the Pharisees or getting upset about the unholy activity going on in God's temple. They were used to it. It was part of their culture.

Similarly, I think we have become much too accustomed to allowing sin to invade the church because it's part of our culture. The culture of the world in the twenty-first century is so self-centered. Whatever you want, you get it. It doesn't matter that you took an oath to be committed to this person; if he or she doesn't make you happy anymore, you have the right to leave. No one has the right to judge you. What matters most is that you love who you are. When we start operating like this in the church, we begin catering our theology to people's desires and ultimately their sin. This kind of attitude is so ugly and offensive to God. We can't do this in the church. Our commitment to the Kingdom must take precedence over culture.

Jesus and the apostles were persecuted because what they said and taught was so countercultural. The culture of our world is just as ugly, if not more so, than it was in Jesus' time. The teaching of the church should be radically different from that of the world. There will be backlash, and church attendance might decline, but the church will be purified.

We need to return to a God-centered theology rather than a human-centered theology, and we need to be willing to flip some tables and suffer for it along the way.

PURSUE JESUS, NOT SUFFERING

While it is so crucial to have the willingness to suffer, we have to be careful in how we live out our theology of suffering. Understand the point of the Scriptures is not asceticism. We are not pursuing suffering just for suffering's sake. We pursue Jesus, and suffering always accompanies Him. As believers, we spend our days pursuing Christ Himself, Christlikeness, and the mission of Christ, none of which can be done apart from suffering. We should be like horses with blinders on, looking only straight ahead at our goal. As we are fixated on and obsessed with our pursuit of Jesus, we know persecution will come at us from all sides.

Part of the reason we have created a culture of non-committal Christianity that avoids suffering is that we don't treasure Him enough. We want Jesus, but there are limits to what we will sacrifice for Him. We want Him, but there are lots of things we want in life. The good news is placed on par with or even below other forms of "good news." "I'm getting married!" "I'm having a child!" "The Giants won the World Series!" "God became flesh, was crucified for our sins, rose from the grave, and is returning to judge the world!" Other kinds of good news stir more emotion than the gospel. Think how insulting that kind of attitude must be to God!

We need to take time to dwell and meditate on the impossibility of the cross. The almighty, all-knowing, all-powerful God who spoke the universe into being sent His Son to die a criminal's death so we could be with Him forever. We get to dwell with Him forever! I don't care how many times you've heard it; if that doesn't cause you to fall on your face in worship, there's something wrong!

It's this kind of eternal mind-set that allows us to keep things in perspective when things get difficult. When we truly understand what Jesus did for us, the sacrifice He made on our behalf, and the incomparable beauty of the eternal life promised to those of us who endure, we can't help but fall in love with Him, to the point where it actually becomes a joy and desire to give our lives to Him in return.

"Indeed, I count everything as loss because of the surpassing worth of knowing Christ Jesus my Lord. For his sake I have suffered the loss of all things and count them as rubbish, in order that I may gain Christ and be found in him, not having a righteousness of my own that comes from the law, but that which comes through faith in Christ, the righteousness from God that depends on

*faith—that I may know him and the power of his
resurrection, and may share his sufferings, becoming
like him in his death, that by any means possible
I may attain the resurrection from the dead."*

Philippians 3:8–11

Look at the passage above and ask yourself whether this describes you and whether this is how others would describe you. The apostle Paul was so obsessed with knowing Jesus he even wanted the fellowship of sharing in Christ's sufferings. Imagine if Jesus was being stretched out and whipped and you were on the other side of Him. You're looking at Jesus, face-to-face just taking it with Him. You would be in excruciating pain, but you could look in His eyes and know you're with the Son of God, the Creator of everything, and you're going through this together. Paul wanted to know Jesus as deeply as possible, even if it required immense suffering.

There's a level of love we can reach where we actually grow to want that. To want that type of intimacy, where you feel as if you are nailed right there next to Him. You could lose everything—your reputation, comforts, possessions—and count that all a bunch of trash, because it's all worthless compared with knowing Christ. Suffering is so important because through it we come to know Jesus more. To know the power of His resurrection. To know the fellowship of His sufferings.

LOVE PEOPLE, NOT SUFFERING

*"If I give away all I have, and if I deliver up my body
to be burned, but have not love, I gain nothing."*

1 Corinthians 13:3

God is clear. Our suffering must be motivated by love. This is the example of the Father (John 3:16) and the Son (15:13). If we sacrifice for any other reason, there's no merit in it. It's not even enough to decide to suffer as a missionary. He wants you to love a people group so much that you are broken over their lostness and sacrifice your life to bring the gospel to them.

When was the last time you sacrificed for someone else's sake? Unless I'm mistaken, isn't that the whole point of the gospel? If this isn't commonplace in your life and you can't think of anyone outside your family you'd sacrifice for, you need to seriously examine your life. This is what separates Christians from the rest of the world. We suffer because we love people, even our enemies.

I have friends who have adopted children because they wanted children. I have other friends who have adopted children because they loved children. There's a big difference. I have friends who love so well they have adopted children with special needs or troubled children out of the foster system. These loving decisions often wreak havoc in a family. As I ask the couples why they do this, the answer usually sounds like this: "We don't think about how much we will suffer if we take her in; we think about how much she will suffer if we don't."

When we love others, we are being the hands and feet of Jesus. Jesus loved the marginalized, rejected, and forgotten. And at the end of His life, His hands and feet were nailed to a cross. Real love demands something of us, and it will lead us into suffering.

NEW EXPECTATIONS

> *"Beloved, do not be surprised at the fiery trial when it comes upon you to test you, as though something strange were happening to you. But rejoice insofar as you share Christ's sufferings, that you may also rejoice and be glad when his glory is revealed. If you are insulted for the name of Christ, you are blessed, because the Spirit of glory and of God rests upon you."*
>
> 1 Peter 4:12–14

This passage says it all! Peter told us not to be surprised when trials come "as though something strange were happening" (v. 12). Trials are part of the plan. Because of a false gospel that many people have been taught, they question God's sovereignty when suffering comes. Scripture says we should expect it. And there should be a part of us that actually wants it so we can "rejoice and be glad when his glory is revealed" (v. 13).

Think about Christ returning in all His glory. Imagine how joyful you would be if you could recall suffering you endured for His sake. Now you could anticipate eternal rewards. Peter said that those of us who have suffered rejection for His sake are "blessed, because the Spirit of glory and of God rests upon you" (v. 14). This is a powerful statement. He was saying your willingness to suffer is proof the Spirit of God rests upon you. Our suffering proves to us that we really are Christians!

Christians are people who believe in life after death. The Church is a Bride that believes the Groom is returning and He is going to take her away to be with Him for all of eternity. Our confidence in this truth produces actions that look stupid to an unbelieving world. Our hope motivates us to suffer. We understand the brevity of life and eagerly hope for a glorious eternity. We are sure of it. We are betting everything on it, even our lives.

The apostle Paul suffered more than anyone I know. In speaking of his personal sacrifice, he said, "If in Christ we have hope in this life only, we are of all people most to be pitied" (1 Cor. 15:19). He knew how idiotic his actions would be if his existence ended at death, but it didn't matter because he was confident his physical death would just be the beginning. The suffering in his life was proof he believed the first verse we all memorized. He knew he would "not perish but have eternal life" (John 3:16). This is the good news. He did not have to fear death or suffering, and neither do we.

So expect suffering, desire it, and rejoice in the midst of it. This is our DNA, our heritage, and God's plan for the Church. We are called to be an army of people who are so madly in love with Jesus that we are unshakable. This is the kind of force that can change the world.

> *"Therefore, since we are surrounded by so great a cloud of witnesses, let us also lay aside every weight, and sin which clings so closely, and let us run with endurance the race that is set before us, looking to Jesus, the founder and perfecter of our faith, who for the joy that was set before him endured the cross, despising the shame, and is seated at the right hand of the throne of God. Consider him who endured from sinners such hostility against himself, so that you may not grow weary or fainthearted."*
>
> Hebrews 12:1–3

Let's arm ourselves with this mind-set. Let's remember heaven and live in light of what's coming. Let's spur on one another to greater levels of surrender and radical expressions of boldness. Let's encourage one another to rejoice in suffering. We want to become Spirit-filled, gospel-centered Christians devoted to prayer; but let's not forget, we also want to be suffering Christians. That's who Jesus was, a suffering servant. Let's endure until the end.

COULD IT BE MORE OBVIOUS?

I am going to close this chapter with Bible verses. I already filled this chapter with plenty of Scripture because I wanted to be clear that this is not some obscure and isolated teaching in the New Testament. It may feel new to you if you attend a church that teaches not the entirety of Scripture but only the parts that are palatable to the masses.

Jesus made it clear that following Him meant suffering, and so did everyone else in the New Testament. So please don't just jump to the next chapter. While reading books, I have been guilty of skimming verses that are familiar to me. Please don't do that here. Take the time to meditate on and pray through the following passages. You could have an amazing time of fellowship with Jesus as you interact with these verses.

*"The Spirit himself bears witness with our spirit
that we are children of God, and if children, then
heirs—heirs of God and fellow heirs with Christ,
provided we suffer with him in order that we may
also be glorified with him. For I consider that the
sufferings of this present time are not worth comparing
with the glory that is to be revealed to us."*
Romans 8:16–18

"Put on the whole armor of God, that you may be able to stand against the schemes of the devil. For we do not wrestle against flesh and blood, but against the rulers, against the authorities, against the cosmic powers over this present darkness, against the spiritual forces of evil in the heavenly places."

Ephesians 6:11–12

"For it has been granted to you that for the sake of Christ you should not only believe in him but also suffer for his sake."

Philippians 1:29

"This is evidence of the righteous judgment of God, that you may be considered worthy of the kingdom of God, for which you are also suffering."

2 Thessalonians 1:5

"Share in suffering as a good soldier of Christ Jesus."

2 Timothy 2:3

"Indeed, all who desire to live a godly life in Christ Jesus will be persecuted."

2 Timothy 3:12

"So Jesus also suffered outside the gate in order to sanctify the people through his own blood. Therefore let us go to him outside the camp and bear the reproach he endured."

Hebrews 13:12–13

"For this is a gracious thing, when, mindful of God, one endures sorrows while suffering unjustly. For what credit is it if, when you sin and are beaten for it, you endure? But if when you do good and suffer for it you endure, this is a gracious thing in the sight of God. For to this you have been called, because Christ also suffered for you, leaving you an example, so that you might follow in his steps."

1 Peter 2:19–21

"Do not be surprised, brothers, that the world hates you."

1 John 3:13

"By this we know love, that he laid down his life for us, and we ought to lay down our lives for the brothers. But if anyone has the world's goods and sees his brother in need, yet closes his heart against him, how does God's love abide in him? Little children, let us not love in word or talk but in deed and in truth."

1 John 3:16–18

*"Do not fear what you are about to suffer.
Behold, the devil is about to throw some of you
into prison, that you may be tested, and for ten
days you will have tribulation. Be faithful unto
death, and I will give you the crown of life."*

Revelation 2:10

UNLEASHED

I was having lunch in São Paulo with the pastor of a thriving congregation. I began encouraging him for the exciting things I saw happening, but he stopped me mid-compliment and said, "Yeah, but the church still feels too much like a zoo. So many churches feel like zoos. We take these powerful animals out of the jungle and put them on display in cages. Have you ever seen the movie *Madagascar*?" I immediately knew what he was talking about.

The movie begins with a bunch of "wild" animals in a zoo. All the spectators are in awe of these powerful and als. Everyone's favorite is the lion; the children eering every time he roars. Most of the animals love this setup. They're extremely well cared for. Trainers wait on them hand and foot, bringing them everything they need and ensuring that their habitats, which are carefully designed to look like "the wild," are safe and comfortable for the animals.

But the zebra finds himself dreaming about the wild. He can't shake the feeling that he wasn't made to live in a zoo; he was made to roam free. His restlessness creates a situation where several of the animals escape the zoo and later find themselves stranded in the jungle of Madagascar. The movie is hilarious, mostly stemming from watching domesticated animals trying to survive in the wild. These animals were born to live free, born with the instincts and physical characteristics required to thrive. But their zoo environment had made them tame, useless in the wild.[1]

I wonder whether you've felt like the zebra. You've been a faithful member of your church, but you keep feeling like you were made for something more. Maybe you've even experienced what it's like to live in the wild. It may have been on an overseas mission trip or while boldly reaching out in your own neighborhood. You've known the joy of seeing your instincts kick in and allow you to thrive. But now you're stuck in the zoo, where everything is comfortable, everything is controlled. And you just want to get back to living in the wild.

LESSONS FROM THE EAST

I was in Seoul at a breakfast for megachurch pastors. One pastor, who was leading a church of seventy thousand people, asked me, "How can I get my people to leave and live by faith?" He explained how he had become really proficient at gathering people together, but his intention was to get them to disperse to share the gospel and live by faith. But now they had grown comfortable and didn't want to leave.

Another pastor of a smaller church ("only" forty thousand people) explained that the founding pastor had told the congregation not to stay in the church longer than five years. In his mind, after five years, there wouldn't be anything else they could learn from him. Like a child turning eighteen, it would be time for them to start a new journey. But they were running into a problem: once the people got comfortable in the zoo, they refused to leave. In fact, they no longer believed they were able to live outside the zoo.

I was in Beijing, speaking to pastors who used to lead underground churches. Now that oppression was easing up in China, they had been given more freedom, so they began taking their churches above ground. They rented buildings and started running services the way we do in America. It was great for a while, but these pastors became so discouraged. I wish I could convey the frustration and desperation in their voices. They talked about the good old days, when their people were risking their lives and radically sharing the gospel, making disciples. But now these pastors were lamenting the way their people attend services and expect the leaders to feed them and cater to them. They had seen this same transition in Korea and were terrified it would happen in their context as well. All anyone wanted was a Jesus and a church that served their needs and kept them comfortable. What started as a movement became a bunch of people sitting safely in services.

My mind flashed back to five years prior when my daughter and I went to an underground gathering in China. Young people were praying so passionately, begging God to send them to the most dangerous places. They were actually hoping to die as martyrs! I had never seen anything like it. I still can't get over the fearless passion for Jesus this church embodied. As they shared stories of persecution, I sat in amazement and asked for more stories. After a while, they asked why I was so intrigued. I told them the church in America was nothing like this. I can't tell you how embarrassing it was to try to explain to them that people attend ninety-minute services once a week in buildings and that's what we call "church." I told them about how people switch churches if they find better teaching, more exciting music, or more robust programs for their kids. As I described church life in America, they began to laugh. Not just small chuckles; they were laughing hysterically. I felt like a stand-up comedian, but I was simply describing the American church as

I've experienced it. They found it laughable that we could read the same Scriptures they were reading and then create something so incongruent.

I was talking to a pastor from the Philippines who has over thirty thousand people in his church. He told me he used to send missionaries to the United States for Bible training but he would never make that mistake again. He explained that once these would-be missionaries spent time in the US, they never came back! Once they tasted the comforts, they came up with all sorts of reasons they were called to take a nice salary from a church and raise their children in America.

Sometimes it takes an outsider to point out glaring issues we have become blind to. This pastor now trains missionaries in the Philippines, in an environment where there's no temptation to stay. It keeps them on mission. In the wild.

HYPOTHETICAL POWER?

When the Bible describes the power available to you, doesn't it sound like hyperbole? It seems so extreme, yet we see so little of this in our own lives and in the Church. The discrepancy could challenge your faith in the Scriptures—how can the Bible promise things we never experience in real life? But are you willing to consider that the Bible is accurate and the Church has domesticated us to the point where we doubt our power?

Perhaps we're all so comfortable in the zoo that we dismiss "the wild" as a myth. Are we sure our churches aren't zoos?

Rather than producing powerful and fearless missionaries who go to the ends of the earth, we are left with thirtysomethings who live in their parents' basements and complain about not having a singles' group. After all, how can a Christian possibly survive outside a singles' cage with weekly feedings? We're busy reassuring one another that God wants us to do what's safest for our families and to pursue God in a way that looks suspiciously similar to what we'd naturally do if our only concern was our own comfort and happiness.

Church, the answer is not to build bigger and nicer cages. Nor is it to renovate the cages so they look more like the wild. It's time to open the cages, remind the animals of their God-given instincts and capabilities, and release them into the wild. Alan Hirsch said, "In so many churches the mission of the church has actually become the maintenance of the institution itself."[2] The way to destroy the victim mentality is not by giving them more but by sending them out.

"[I pray you would know] what is the immeasurable
greatness of his power toward us who believe, according
to the working of his great might that he worked
in Christ when he raised him from the dead and

seated him at his right hand in the heavenly places,
far above all rule and authority and power and
dominion, and above every name that is named,
not only in this age but also in the one to come."

Ephesians 1:19–21

Take a close look at the words "immeasurable greatness of his power" (v. 19). When is the last time someone reminded you of this truth? It is similar to what Paul said in Ephesians 3:20: "Now to him who is able to do far more abundantly than all that we ask or think, according to the power at work within us."

Name three people you know who live as if they believe this.

This was meant for us all. But it isn't something we can just teach in a sermon. This type of faith requires real prayer. We need to spend less time catering to the felt needs of people and spend more time praying Paul's prayers in Ephesians 1 and 3. We need more solid Bible teaching to remind them of these deeper truths so they don't run to shallow pleasures or cling to familiar comforts.

We are capable of so much more. We are like ferocious beasts who were made for the wild. When we gather as the Church, we are supposed to "stir up one another to love and good works" (Heb. 10:24). Don't get me wrong—it's fun to watch a lion eat a piece of meat the zookeeper throws at him, but it's pretty lame compared with watching a lion hunt in the wild. It's time to train people to live in the wild again. Even our gatherings should feel wild (while remaining orderly). Read through the kinds of things happening in the churches in Acts and 1 Corinthians 12–14. They were urged to remain orderly, but God was doing some crazy things through the Church.

How would you describe your gatherings? I'm guessing *wild* isn't applicable.

KEEP THE CHILDREN AWAY

I've never said that phrase out loud, but I did actually put a sign in the church lobby saying kids under five years old were not allowed in the sanctuary. We encouraged kids under twelve to be in kids' programs rather than with the adults. I think I had good motives. I didn't want the infants and toddlers to distract, and I felt the kids could get more from a program made specifically for them. I still believe we have to be mindful of those factors, but there's a bigger story here.

If the Holy Spirit enters a person at salvation, do the believing children receive a full version of the Holy Spirit? If so, do they have gifts meant to build up the body? Notice the shockingly strong language Jesus used when He spoke about children in Matthew 18.

After telling the disciples to allow the children to come close to Him, Jesus made the following statements. I picture the kids surrounding Him, maybe sitting on His lap as He taught the adults, saying, "Unless you turn and become like children, you will never enter the kingdom of heaven" (v. 3).

I'm not sure you can make a stronger statement than that. It should produce trembling rather than warm feelings about a cute kids' verse. If our entrance into heaven is predicated on our childlikeness, shouldn't that cause us to pay close attention to children in order to imitate them? Jesus went on to say,

> *"Whoever humbles himself like this child is the greatest*
> *in the kingdom of heaven. Whoever receives one such*
> *child in my name receives me, but whoever causes one*
> *of these little ones who believe in me to sin, it would be*
> *better for him to have a great millstone fastened around*
> *his neck and to be drowned in the depth of the sea."*
>
> Matthew 18:4–6

Could Jesus' language be any harsher? And He used this strong language to speak against those who mistreat—or even undervalue—children!

"See that you do not despise one of these little ones," Jesus said. "For I tell you that in heaven their angels always see the face of my Father who is in heaven" (v. 10). There is some debate about precisely what "their angels" is referring to. Regardless of the exact meaning, this is a severe warning to people like me who can too easily get irritated by disobedient kids.

Jesus insisted, "It is not the will of my Father who is in heaven that one of these little ones should perish" (v. 14). Right before Jesus said this, He spoke about the one lost sheep as opposed to the ninety-nine safely within the fold. Read it in context. Did you know He was talking about children in that passage?

God values children and their role in His Kingdom far more than we do. We need to repent of this and do all we can to value their contribution. God sees them as far more than an obligation or inconvenience. In my setting, these passages have led us to incorporate our children into our gatherings, and the results have been powerful. Listening to the kids talk about what they learn from their devotions is uplifting and encouraging. Having the kids pray over the adults has been humbling and powerful. The faith of their prayers and the simplicity in their sharing accomplish something adults cannot pull off.

LESSONS FROM AFRICA

My friend Jen leads a ministry that currently disciples over 250,000 children in Africa on a weekly basis. These children actually go into unreached people groups, heal the sick, and preach the gospel. Kids! Last year (2017), these children shared the gospel with 169 unreached people groups. They are sharing the gospel in places where adult missionaries have been killed for trying to spread the gospel. There are stories of God doing things through them we could never imagine Him doing through us.

Jen tells me of how these kids went into a village where there was great spiritual darkness. Children in the village died mysteriously every week and no one could figure out why. The kids fearlessly stayed in the village and prayed for hours. The entire situation lifted because of their prayers, and children in the village stopped dying mysterious deaths. Many in the village were led to Jesus. There are many other stories of children going in simple faith to heal animists and Muslims in the name of Jesus. Don't you find it even a bit discouraging that these kids are transforming villages while our kids are watching puppet shows on Jonah and learning songs with hand motions? Are you sure this is what we have to settle for because of our geographic location? It could be that we have been wasting our most precious resource. It could be that we have been treating our greatest assets as obligations.

RELEASE THE CHILDREN

We need to start reminding our children of their power. Maybe it's our lack of expectation from younger kids that bleeds into the way we treat middle-school kids in the church. We teach them as if their only goal is to refuse to drink or have sex. Then when they hit high school, we try to entertain them enough so they keep coming. A far cry from the one lost sheep! We can keep doing things the way we've always done them, but maybe we need to do more releasing and less taming. What would happen if we trained our young lions to attack rather than keep them sheltered? It's time we obey Jesus' words and set ourselves in the posture of learning from our kids.

I have been a father long enough to know that there are no perfect, one-size-fits-all answers to parenting. Parenting is one of the most difficult things you can pursue. So please understand I am not saying my way is the right way. I just want to add to the conversation. I am amazed by each of my kids, but I don't dare take credit for their faith or accomplishments. Any good in my children is 100 percent by the grace of God and the power of the Holy Spirit in them. I believe this and thank God often for saving and empowering my kids.

Having said this, there has been a significant shift among Christian parents toward homeschooling. I'm not saying this is inherently bad. All my children have gone to public school thus far, but that doesn't mean we will continue public schooling. I just have to say that I have seen God use my children in powerful ways in the public school. Far beyond just keeping their virginity or staying away from drugs and alcohol, the Spirit has used them in great ways. We have seen them share the gospel, lead friends to Jesus, and stand for truth before classrooms. They have challenged teachers and brought several into the Church. None of this should surprise us if we believe in the Holy Spirit.

Some say it's unfair to throw a child into a public school. They compare it to throwing a kid into a rushing river to teach him or her to swim. It's unfair and impossible. That assumes the Holy Spirit has limited or no power in their lives. I have chosen to see my children as Olympic swimmers. I tell them they are missionaries in their schools and can trust in the Spirit's power to overcome challenges and to have an impact on those around them. My hope is this training in Holy Spirit dependence proves helpful in an unreached people group or Fortune 500 company.

Again, I am not saying everyone should throw their kids into public school. I am also not saying we should foolishly endanger them. I am just wondering whether our habit of underestimating God's power in them may be a mind-set we develop in them that continues through middle school, high school, and into adulthood. Maybe our lack of courage took a while to develop.

RELEASE THE PEOPLE

As I've been writing about children, I'm really not just talking about children. Our kids are simply a case in point for the way we function in the Church. We underestimate them, and we're afraid of what will happen if we let them loose, so we keep them entertained, educated, and insulated. Is this really any different from the way we treat the average member of our churches?

Of course, when we structure our churches like this, it's not just the children or the average folks we are underestimating—it's the Holy Spirit! We've built our modern churches on the assumption that God works through a few talented, impressive, and wealthy people. And we give all the other people a comfortable seats from which they can be blessed by what God does through these leaders and influencers.

I honestly believe we in the American Church need to get on our knees and repent of our condescending attitudes toward God's Holy Spirit. We have read Scripture's clear statements about the Spirit manifesting Himself through every Christian, but we've decided we know better, these people aren't ready for anything serious, and it will be more effective if the talented few do all the heavy lifting. We don't believe the Spirit is capable of working through the people around us. We believe we are wiser. May God forgive us for building our church empires on the foundation of our own arrogance!

Don't get me wrong—our zoos are impressive. The animals have really learned to be at home in their habitats. In many cases, an audience member might feel as if he or she is really in the wild! But we know there's something more. We know we weren't made for cages. It's time to stop building and maintaining zoos. It's time for us to figure out what it means to be the Church in the wild.

SENDING

Only months after calling His disciples, Jesus sent them out. This doesn't mean they were fully trained and mistake free. It shows that sending was part of their training. Jesus didn't teach them in a classroom setting. They walked with Him, and they were sent out by Him. He expected them to proclaim repentance, cast out demons, and heal (Mark 6:12–13). He told them He was sending them out as sheep among wolves and explained that they would be hated and persecuted (Matt. 10:16–22) It was also at this time that Jesus promised they would be given words to say during their most trying times. It was an extremely dangerous mission they were sent on with minimal training.

Maybe this is why these men were able to make disciples around the world. This is the opposite of how we train people today! Should we consider that placing people in comfortable classrooms and auditoriums for years may not be the best way to train fearless leaders? Consider some of the movements that have happened recently in other countries. This is all due to a belief that training and sending is for everyone.

Look at the following stats:[3]

- "In East Asia, a missionary reported: 'I launched my three-year plan in November, 2000. My vision was to see 200 new churches started among my people group over the next three years. But four months later, we had already reached that goal. After only six months, we had already seen 360 churches planted and more than 10,000 new believers baptized! Now I'm asking God to enlarge my vision.'"

- "Chinese Christians in Qing'an County of Heilongjiang Province planted 236 new churches in a single month." In 2002 a church planting movement in China brought about 15,000 new churches and baptized 160,000 new believers in one year.

- "During the decade of the 1990s, Christians in a Latin American country overcame relentless government persecution to grow from 235 churches to more than 4,000 churches with more than 30,000 converts awaiting baptism."

- "After centuries of hostility to Christianity, many Central Asian Muslims … are embracing the gospel. In Kazakhstan, [the decade before 2004 saw] more than 13,000 Kazakhs come to faith, worshipping in more than 300 new Kazakh churches."

- "A missionary … in Africa reported: 'It took us 30 years to plant four churches in this country. We've started 65 new churches in the last nine months.'"

- In the heart of India, in the state Madhya Pradesh, one movement planted 4,000 new churches in less than seven years. Elsewhere in India, "in the decade of the 1990s, the Kui people of Orissa started nearly 1,000 new churches.... In 1999, they baptized more than 8,000 new believers. By 2001 they were starting a new church every 24 hours."
- In Outer Mongolia, a church planting movement saw more than 10,000 new followers. Another movement in Inner Mongolia counted more than 50,000 new believers—all during the 1990s.

Don't we all want to be a part of movements like these? This is the kind of power we would expect to see among believers. It makes sense in light of Scripture.

The Church was meant to be a beautiful army, sent out to shed light throughout the earth. Rather than hiding together in a bunker, we were supposed to fearlessly take His message to the most remote places. People should be in awe when they see His people with a peace that surpasses comprehension and rejoicing with an inexpressible joy (Phil. 4:7; 1 Pet. 1:8). Think about what those passages are saying! Once again, those phrases sound like exaggerations rather than expectations. Have people ever been in disbelief over the amount of peace you display? Are you known for being ridiculously joyful? Add that to "the immeasurable greatness of his power" in you (Eph. 1:19) and you cannot go unnoticed. We have tried to attract people through so many different strategies. What if they saw an army of people with inexpressible joy, peace that surpasses comprehension, and immeasurable greatness of power? How could they not be intrigued?

People were attracted to the early church. Who wouldn't be fascinated by a group that shared possessions, rejoiced nonstop, had peace beyond comprehension and immeasurable power, never complained, always gave thanks …? Some people joined them, others hated them, but few could ignore them. They wouldn't allow people to ignore them as they went out fearlessly sharing the gospel. This is our heritage. This is in our DNA. We must stop creating safe places for people to hide and start developing fearless warriors to send out.

CHURCH AGAIN

If I could go back and hand a note to the twenty-five-year-old version of me, here are some things I would write:

"Definitely marry Lisa. You won't regret it."

"Have plenty of kids. And don't stress about your oldest—she ends up fine."

"Know God. Don't just serve Him. You tend to spend your time accomplishing tasks. God wants you to sit with Him. It's not a waste of time."

"When you start your church, don't just copy others. Study the Bible with fresh eyes, and search for what He actually commands. You will be constantly tempted to do what you want or what others want. Do what pleases God most. The years will fly by faster than you can imagine. You are going to face God sooner than you know, so don't let people talk you out of your convictions."

We would all do things differently if we could go back and relive the last twenty-five years. One of the blessings in my life is that I actually had an opportunity to start over. God gave me a chance to start another church, and the older (hopefully wiser) me is approaching Church much differently than the younger me did. We are still far from what I believe the Church can become, but I am loving the process.

While part of me wishes I had spent my whole life doing things this way, I also see how God used the path I took for His glory. In hindsight, I see how God used even my pride for His purposes. When Cornerstone was growing, some pastors tried to convince me that growing smaller churches was a better strategy for cultivating the love and obedience God wanted. In my arrogance, I thought to myself, *They are only going small because they are incapable of building a large church and their vision isn't as big as mine. It's great they are being faithful with the three talents they have been given. I need to be faithful with the eight or nine talents He has given me.* That is so embarrassing to publicly admit, but maybe some will find my confession helpful. There is a prevailing attitude that the best thing we can do is build the largest church we are capable of building.

Maybe my flawed journey can dispel notions that going small is merely the default of the less competent and show that it can actually be a choice made out of biblical conviction and a desire to reach the masses.

I went back and forth trying to decide whether I even wanted to write this chapter. Up to this point, the book has been about biblical absolutes. I have addressed sin issues that no church can afford to ignore. These are clear commands from the mouth of God. You would be crazy to see failure in these areas and do nothing.

I don't want to confuse the issue now by writing about my current church experience, but I know there are a lot of people who are curious how we try to flesh out these commands in twenty-first-century America. The purpose of this chapter is to describe some things we have done in an effort to be obedient to the commands mentioned in the previous chapters. Those commands are perfect and holy, and my hope in this book is simply to motivate you to change anything necessary in order to be obedient.

If our church in San Francisco grows to one hundred thousand people, then you shouldn't be motivated more. And if it shrinks to a dozen people, then you shouldn't be motivated less. God's commands are sacred. They came from the mouth of God. That should be more than enough to motivate our tireless pursuit of obedience. If one of my pastors suddenly has a moral failure next week (God forbid), it doesn't negate the truth of everything that has been written thus far. Okay, I think I've made enough disclaimers. You get the point.

STRUCTURE MATTERS

The New Testament avoids laying out a model for precisely how the Church ought to be structured. The biblical authors could have been very clear on this, but instead, they leave us with a lot of freedom. I think that's important, and it's part of preserving the mystery of the Church.

This doesn't mean that structure does not matter. I have learned from years of attending and pastoring churches that we have to be intentional about the way we structure our churches, because it dictates the direction the church will go. Solid, biblical structure is absolutely necessary to keep us from going astray.

Your church model often communicates your true theology. In reexamining what the Church was meant to be, Tim Chester and Steve Timmis borrowed the concept of "heretical structures" from John Stott. Here's how this works. I'm assuming your church's doctrinal statement says something about every believer using his or her spiritual gifts to manifest the Holy Spirit. That's good theology. But let me ask you this: Does your church structure convey a different theology? Does your structure demonstrate that the gift of every believer matters? Or does it suggest that only the gifts of the teaching pastor, a couple ministry leaders, and a few musicians matter? If so, you're functioning with a heretical structure. Your heretical structure almost certainly speaks louder than your orthodox theological statement. "The theology that matters is not the theology we profess but the theology we practice."[1]

I continue to run into people who assume certain modern traditions are necessities. The reality is that some of these optional practices can actually hinder the Church from living out the biblical principles meant to shape the Church. There are elements of modern churches that on the surface seem like good ideas, but they can actually keep us from the biblical vision of unity, true fellowship, mutual love, and pursuit of the mission. Too many look at these elements and insist you can't have a church without them.

MORE ROOM FOR GOD

As I write this, my wife is in the garage. I can hear her clearing the shelves of stuff we have accumulated over the past few years. I love it when we purge. Sometimes it actually feels as if I can breathe better when clutter is removed. Maybe you've seen an episode or two of *Hoarders*? It's suffocating to watch people accumulate so much junk they can barely walk in their own homes. Haven't there been times when you have felt suffocated by the busyness at a Christian event?

Something in you longs for more space to breathe, more room for God to move.

I recently took my family on vacation. For four days, we lived in a cabin in the snow. I made a rule for our vacation: no electronics. No phones, video games, TVs, or computers. I know what some of you are thinking: *How did you survive? How did you convince your whole family to live like savages for four whole days?* My rule wasn't exactly met with cheers of celebration, but they knew Dad's intentions. As I expected, the absence of electronic devices forced us to entertain one another. The days were filled with snowball fights, sledding, snowboarding, building fires, playing board games, talking, laughing—you know, all the things humans used to do before we discovered smartphones. As you probably guessed, we had an absolute blast and came home more bonded as a family. In fact, some of the kids suggested we do this on every vacation! By removing electronic devices, we made more room for one another.

I think we would be surprised by how much more we would experience if we had less. Imagine if the Church purged until all that was left was a group of people with a Bible, a cup, and some bread. For some that sounds boring; for others it sounds ideal. For many around the world, that is all they have ever known of Church and they love it. We might all benefit from a simpler experience of Church. It would lead to deeper relationships and a stronger dependence on God. We might find that the things we added to improve our churches are the very things that crowd God out.

Some of our additions are birthed from a lack of faith. We don't really expect God to move, so we fill our gatherings with exciting elements that will entertain people even if God does nothing. This won't work in the long run. Eventually the people will no longer be amused with the type of excitement they can find at the movies. They came to the Church to find something otherworldly. Don't be afraid of silence. Don't be afraid to develop gatherings that will be dull if God doesn't move. Days of praying together in an upper room require faith and patience, but the payoff will be worth it. We have to stop assuming that bigger and busier is always better than smaller and simpler. We can't keep increasing production as a substitute for genuine expressions of the Spirit in ordinary, nonprofessional people.

WE ARE CHURCH BEGINNINGS

In 2013 I gathered about twenty people at my house. I didn't have a detailed plan, just a lot of convictions. At our first gathering, I remember saying I wanted us to be focused on pursuing everything I saw in the New Testament. I wanted to see deep familial love and for all of us to be using our gifts. I made it clear that I would not be the pastor forever. Instead, during the six to twelve months I led the church, I would disciple four people and help them become pastors so when our church multiplied into two churches, each church would be led by two of the pastors I had discipled.

We became such a tight family that everyone hated when it came time to multiply, but we understood it was necessary so we could grow and produce more leaders.

We have made many changes over the years, and I anticipate more. While the church will be in constant change, the elders have tried to keep us focused on some core values. Though the wording has changed over time, this is basically what we are striving to produce.

Devoted Worshippers. We want to be people who are committed to worshipping God, people who can't get enough of Him, not people who worship only when it is convenient or when the right people are leading. It must be the Object of our worship that makes worshipping exciting to us.

Loving Families. We want to be people who love one another deeply and show this by how we sacrifice for one another. Our goal is not merely to get along but to love one another to the extent that Christ loved us and to be united to the extent that the Father is one with the Son.

Equipped Disciple Makers. We want everyone trained up to make disciples. No one should come as a consumer, but we need everyone to come as a servant using his or her gifts to build up the body.

Spirit-Filled Missionaries. We want to be people with supernatural character, who regularly share the gospel with neighbors and coworkers. Some will go to foreign countries to share Christ where He has not been heard. The others will support those who have gone.

Suffering Sojourners. We want to be people who are eagerly waiting for the return of Christ. We are willing and wanting to suffer because we believe in heavenly rewards. Far from seeking comfort, we thrive on hardship, refusing to become citizens of this earth.

This is what we are after as a church. We don't want to get caught up in anything that will distract us from these things. For this reason, we have a few daily and weekly practices. As I said earlier, structure matters. It's easy to say these are our values, but unless we structure in weekly practices to achieve these goals and structure out anything that distracts, we will never become the church we want to be.

Below are some of the practices we have found helpful in achieving our values.

Daily Bible Readings. We want people to be obsessed with Jesus. We believe the most effective way of cultivating this is by spending time alone with God in the Scriptures daily. Our members follow the same reading plan, which enables us to talk about the Scriptures with one another daily.[2]

Meet in Homes. There are more than fifty "one another" commands that call us to care for one another in a supernatural way. God wants meaningful interactions when we gather. For this reason, we keep our churches small (ten to twenty people), meeting in homes to create a family atmosphere. This way each person can be known and use his or her gifts to bless others.

Multiply Leaders. In Luke 10:2, Jesus told His disciples to pray that God would send more workers out into the world. For this reason, we pray and constantly develop new pastors and elders to be sent out. Each church has two pastors, who train future pastors for the next church plant. Pastors are the spiritual parents of the congregation, having both the responsibility and the authority.

Elder Authority. Some of you have experienced a form of home churches where the leader is rebelling against authority and simply doing what he or she wants to do. That's not healthy. The size of the church has nothing to do with this point. As we have seen, God designed His Church to function under the leadership and humble, service-oriented authority of elders (1 Pet. 5:1–4). At a time when everyone bashes leadership, God calls us to show the world something different: people who love having a King and joyfully follow godly leaders.

Everyone Discipled. It is the Church's responsibility to bring people to maturity (Eph. 4:11–16). Jesus set a wonderful example of living life with His disciples. We expect every member to have a more mature believer shepherding him or her toward maturity and greater holiness.

Everyone Disciples. Jesus rose from the dead and then commanded His followers to make disciples (Matt. 28:16–20). He was calling them to share the good news with those who didn't know Him, teaching them to obey His commands. We want all our members to share the gospel with those who don't believe and to teach them to become disciple makers.

Everyone Exercises Gifts. Paul said, "To each is given the manifestation of the Spirit for the common good" (1 Cor. 12:7). He went on to list various gifts and emphasized the necessity of each member. We create space for everyone to contribute at gatherings and in everyday life. We aim for total participation, where each member blesses others with his or her gifts.

Regular Multiplication of Churches. We must stay focused on reaching those who don't know Jesus (Acts 1:8). It is so easy for house churches to become selfish rather than missional. We naturally run toward comfort. Our churches aim to multiply annually to maintain a healthy pressure toward developing leaders and reaching more people. Let's face it: without deadlines, not much gets done.

Simple Gatherings. The early church "devoted themselves to the apostles' teaching and the fellowship, to the breaking of bread and the prayers" (Acts 2:42). We want the same. We want believers excited to break bread and wonder at the mystery of His body. We want people thrilled to come before a holy God in prayer. So we work hard to keep from adding elements to our gatherings that could distract us from what we must be devoted to.

Share Possessions. "And all who believed were together and had all things in common. And they were selling their possessions and belongings and distributing the proceeds to all, as any had need" (Acts 2:44–45). The early church was known for how they cared for one another. They focused on eternity and cared little about earthly possessions. We joyfully share our resources as we learn of needs locally and around the world (2 Cor. 8:1–15).

Assume Missions. God wants to be worshipped by every nation and language (Rev. 7:9–10). There are still billions who have never heard the gospel.[3] For this reason, we ask everyone to consider going to unreached people groups. Rather than assuming you are staying until you hear a word from God, it seems more biblical to assume you are going unless you believe God called you to stay.

I don't believe we have found *the* solution for the future church, only *a* solution. But the changes we've made have felt more like the New Testament Church than anything I've ever encountered in the States. Again, I'm not trying to push the model we've been running with, but I do think we'd all benefit from innovative thinking where we jump back to the essentials, forget about "what we've always done," and ask what expressions of Church God wants to see in our setting.

WHY GO SMALL?

I believe God is leading a movement in this country toward simple, smaller gatherings, and I long to see this movement gain greater traction. I get so excited when I dream about the Church spreading in small, invigorating expressions that look and feel like the early church. My goal is to get you dreaming about this as well.

Recently the president of a well-known missions agency was sharing his concerns about the current state of missions. His burden was that we have been sticking to our old methods even though the unreached world has changed. Why are we still training missionaries to build churches when most of the unreached live in countries where it is illegal to plant a church? He shared about the desperate need for Christians to have an impact on closed countries. The only way this can happen is if we expand our narrow church experience. Our parameters for church expression must revert back to what is biblical rather than sticking to what is normal at this cultural moment. If we continue to promote a model where people flood to a church building to congregate around a preacher, how do we expect to reach the billions of people who live where that model is illegal?

If our missionaries have to reject everything we've ever taught them about Church in order to reach another country, are we confident what we're doing here is best? Whether or not you believe smaller gatherings are the best method of church planting in the States, pretty much everyone agrees it's the only way to plant churches in many countries. But how do we expect to successfully send people to plant churches if their only experience is the traditional model?

A CASE FOR CHURCHBNB

One leader I talked to used the Hyatt hotel chain as an illustration. In 2015 Hyatt had 97,000 employees.[4] By contrast, Airbnb had 2,300.[5] Yet Airbnb had far more rooms available than Hyatt! In fact, three years later they have more rooms available than the top five hotel chains combined![6] How did they do this? They put the hotel industry into the hands of the everyday person. Not everyone has the ability to raise tens of millions of dollars to buy land and build a luxury hotel. But anyone with a smartphone can now rent out a room in his or her house. They rapidly grew to four million listings without building a single facility!

The Church needs to learn from this. When you're caught in a long-standing model or structure, any alternative seems laughable. But history is full of models, companies, and inventions that became obsolete almost overnight because someone dreamed of a revolutionary new way to do something. The new thing always seems to be simpler and more efficient with fewer barriers to entry.

So what would a revolution in church structure look like? What are the inefficiencies and unnecessary appendages we're blind and numb to? What would happen if we put the Church back into the hands of the ordinary Christian? Could we see exponential growth at a fraction of the cost? Is Churchbnb possible?

I believe it's possible because it has been happening overseas for years, and it has been steadily increasing throughout the US. In San Francisco, we have been experimenting with churches led by Christians with full-time jobs. These are professionals in the workplace who pastor small churches out of their homes. These leaders can now transplant anywhere in the world without any need to raise support. They know how to work and pastor at the same time. They know how to work hard and well in the workplace while having a natural setting to build friendships with those who don't know Jesus. This has possibilities in any city in America as well as any city on earth. Not only have we found Churchbnb to be possible, but it also provides a practical solution to many of the problems facing the traditional model of church.

THE POTENTIAL TO GROW AND THE FREEDOM TO DECLINE

Buildings can limit a church's growth. If God wants to move powerfully and save thousands, they won't fit. Buildings also limit a church's ability to decline. If God wants to prune the church, we won't be able to pay the bills. If our church model requires God to work within a narrow "sweet spot," something's wrong. I can't tell you how much freedom I feel now that I'm ministering in a church with no salaries and no potential for any of us to be pastoring a large church. (We try to multiply our churches as soon as they hit twenty people.)

I remember when Cornerstone moved from a two-hundred-seat sanctuary to a four-hundred-seat sanctuary. It was an exciting time. We could all fit comfortably in two services. That lasted for maybe a few months. Then came the third service, then the fourth, fifth, sixth, and satellite services. In less than a year, we were looking for more land or an expansion of our campus.

After years of working with the city and raising funds to build a thousand-seat sanctuary, we moved in. It was an exciting time. We could all fit comfortably in two services. That lasted for a few months. Then came the third, fourth, fifth …

Sound familiar?

Each time I went through this, I thought to myself, *There's no way Jesus would do it this way!* Would He really halt Kingdom growth until He found more land, appeased the city officials, raised money, and built a bigger place? It never made sense to me, but I couldn't think of any other options at the time.

We eventually decided to buy a giant plot of land and worked on plans for the three-thousand-seat meeting area. Then another problem arose in my mind. What if we spend a fortune on the huge sanctuary and thousands of people don't show up? How would we pay the bills? Would I feel pressured to keep the sanctuary filled in order to keep the budget afloat? Then my ego gets involved. I hate empty seats. Would this cause me to avoid controversial topics and become more political? Paul told Timothy, "The time is coming when people will not endure sound teaching, but having itching ears they will accumulate for themselves teachers to suit their own passions" (2 Tim. 4:3). What would I do if people began to be turned off by sound doctrine? We would have wasted millions of dollars to build a sanctuary that never filled up. We'd get behind on the payments without enough satisfied givers, and we'd lose it all!

The alternative is worse—I could preach more politically to keep the masses coming. Not to be dramatic, but I would honestly rather die. I have seriously prayed for God to take me off this earth before He allowed me to dishonor His name, and that would include teaching aimed to please the crowds rather than God Himself.

This was hard enough in Simi Valley; now take into consideration the big cities in our nation. Have you ever tried to purchase a large building in a big city? Price out a building that would seat a thousand people in New York City. Even if you could raise the money, the population of New York is 8,537,673.[7] What's your plan for the other 8,536,673? Let's say the Lord wanted to save 10 percent of the city. Even if you had the billions of dollars to spend, is there room to build enough sanctuaries? Of course not!

Meanwhile, everyone has a home. If it's possible for a church to fit in a home, then we have an infinite number of potential churches no matter where we go. Going small is our best shot at getting big.

If we don't consider the possibility of multiplying smaller churches, we have given up on the big cities. We have to at least try. Our current plan shows that we don't expect God to reach more than 1 percent of the population of the large cities. We must be open to new ways of doing things. Or we can just keep highlighting a couple of "large churches" on the covers of our Christian magazines and pretend we are making a dent.

We all know our world is changing. If we built our current church models on a society that has now changed significantly, why do we assume we must simply keep doing what we've always done? Blindly insisting on our current models might not be that different from trying to maintain a Blockbuster video store in the age of Netflix. I'm obviously not arguing that we change the gospel or water down the truth. I'm simply asking us to reconsider the vehicle we use to deliver it. I'm not even trying to argue that we "keep up with the times." I'm actually calling all of us to go back to Scripture and recover what we've lost. If we find ourselves lost on a detour, why not go back to the right path?

$$$$$$$$$$

One of the greatest advantages of this method is that it requires no budget. It can be completely free. As the churches take offerings, 100 percent of the money can go to the poor and to missions.

From surveys I have studied, it costs on average approximately $1,000 per person annually to attend a church in America.[8] That is, if you divide a church's annual budget (say $100,000) by the number of members (say 100), it comes to $1,000 per person. Depending on location, that number goes up or down. I recently tried to help a church where it cost closer to $3,000 per person to attend. Do the math for my family of nine!

I recognize that I grew up poor, so I have a habit of always trying to find the least expensive way of doing things. I know I can go to extremes, but even a less frugal person must have a hard time reconciling one hundred million Chinese being the Church for free while our American system costs $1,000 a head.

This is not solely about waste; it's also about sustainability. With each economic downturn, churches shut their doors, never to reopen. With one change to the US tax code, many churches would instantly fold. It doesn't seem wise to champion only one structure of church that requires a strong economy or specific tax incentives. If a widespread loss of wealth could eliminate our current church expressions overnight, what does that say about our model?

Let's not forget that as you read this, there are heartbreaking things happening throughout our world. Families are desperately seeking clean water for survival, people are starving, kids are enslaved and being raped. These are tragedies the Church can significantly reduce if we were willing to worship more simply. The financial consideration is a major one. The goal is not saving money just to save money but to literally save lives.

NOWHERE TO HIDE

Another major advantage to the smaller gathering style is that it encourages people who would get lost in the background of a bigger church to come to the forefront. When people see there are no professionals, they are more likely to step up and use the gifts they have. It promotes greater levels of investment and contribution from those present if there isn't a church staff paid to do it for them.

Also, in a gathering of thousands of people, it would be impossible for that congregation to know one another intimately and overwhelming to try. The smaller setting naturally lends itself to greater intimacy. It also makes it possible for everyone to be discipled and for members to hold one another accountable, pray for one another by name, and live like family during the week.

What would be a headache to attempt in the traditional model is natural in this kind of environment.

IS IT TIME FOR A CHANGE?

From the very beginning, the Church has always needed pruning. We've always needed reformers and reformations to speak with the voice of the prophet, to call us back to what we were meant to be. Church history is full of reformations of all sizes that have pulled God's people closer to God's intention for His Church.

After Christianity became the official state religion of Rome in the wake of Constantine (c. AD 300), the Church became a place of privilege and prestige. People would buy their way into church leadership because this was the way to gain power in society. So God raised up a group of monks who exposed the Church's wickedness and greed by pursuing God simply and passionately.

When the Catholic Church went so far astray in the sixteenth century that forgiveness of sins was supposedly being sold by the church and human effort was deemed necessary to salvation, God raised up Martin Luther, who himself stood in a long line of reformers like John Wycliffe and Jan Hus, to call God's people back to a true understanding of grace. When this Reformation became too institutionalized, God raised up Anabaptists to bring reformation to a Church that had already been reformed. There are so many reform movements throughout history: the Celtics, the Moravians, the Azusa Street Revival, the Jesus People. Virtually every denomination we have today began as some sort of reform movement meant to pull the Church closer to God's intention.

There's a part of me that fears becoming overly dramatic, comparing ourselves to the Moravians or Reformers. But they were just people! Why not us? I believe this generation can kill the consumer mind-set in the Church and replace it with a servant attitude that thrives on suffering for His name. There is no reason we can't join with those who have gone before us and be the ones who restore the missional focus of the Church. What else would you rather do with your days?

It should not feel out of the ordinary, harsh, or inappropriate to call the Church to change. Nor should we imagine that our unique expression of Church is the only one God sanctions. Instead, we should be constantly seeking renewal, being ready at any moment to discard the elements of Church that lead us away from God's heart rather than toward it.

Maybe you should do Churchbnb. Maybe you shouldn't. I can't answer that for you. My hope is simply to convince you that there are compelling ways of living as the Church that look nothing like our traditional models. My goal is to get you dreaming, to keep you from settling, to affirm that nagging sense you can't shake that God wants something more for His Church than what you're experiencing.

As we have been stepping out in faith in San Francisco, we have seen encouraging signs of growth. People rarely talk about a great "sermon" but often discuss what they've discovered in their Bible readings. Fellowship over the Word has become normal. People regularly take hours and even days to be alone in the presence of Christ. They enjoy Him. Prayer gatherings go longer than planned, and rarely are people anxious to leave. Families are opening up their homes to others. They give away cars, possessions, and money out of love. It is perfectly normal for accomplished professionals to be best friends with ex-cons. Homeless addicts have become faithful pastors. When we gather, many come with prayer requests for people they've shared the gospel with that week. We recently emptied out all our church bank accounts (we actually took a picture of them all being at $0) to fund the kids' ministry in Africa—over $300,000 was given by people who don't have much! People are sacrificing better living conditions to move closer to the projects. Some are being slandered and betrayed yet rejoicing through it. We have around forty pastors now who work full-time jobs. They are missionaries at work and they shepherd and disciple in their free time. We have plenty of problems, but there is plenty of life.

We seem to be seeing more and more of what pleases God most.

This takes me back to where I started this book. I have never been more in love with Jesus or the Church than I am right now. And the intimacy I've been experiencing with God has been directly tied to my connection with the Church. We still have so far to go, but I can honestly say my experience with the Church no longer looks drastically different from what I read about in Scripture. God does not intend for that to be the exception; it's simply what the Church was meant to be.

I have traveled and seen God's Church multiply and thrive in ways I only dreamed were possible. Now I'm starting to experience it myself. But I never would have experienced this if I had given in to the powerful inertia that pulled me to fall in line with everyone else's expectations.

ARE YOU SURE THIS WILL WORK?

When I talk to people about this, they always ask, "Will it work?" I don't even know what that question means. Do they mean, "Will people show up?" Or "Will they like it?" Or more practically, "Will your church grow?"

These are actually the wrong questions to ask. Jesus never used these things as metrics of success.

Paul actually told Timothy that teaching sound doctrine will not "work"; in fact, it will drive people away (2 Tim.

4:1–5). Yet he was commanded to preach truth because it is what God wants!

Remember, it's not about what I would like, what others would like, or what "works." Church is for Him.

Having said that, I think we would be surprised. We may find that people are actually attracted to a group devoted to the presence of God. After all, it was enough to attract over a hundred million people to the underground church in China. It could be that God is waiting for a group of people to strip away all they think will work and devote themselves to what He commanded.

"Nevertheless, when the Son of Man
comes, will he find faith on earth?"

Luke 18:8

WHERE THE SPIRIT LEADS

I'm sure you have a ton of unanswered questions at this point. That might be a good thing. You are welcome to dig around our website (wearechurch.com) to get more info, but that might be the worst thing you could do. It is usually easier to copy others than to seek God. As I have been insisting, I'm not offering this chapter as a prescription of what I believe every church needs to follow. It just didn't seem right to lay out everything I've written in this book and then refuse to share some of what we have been doing in San Francisco. This may be the very thing God wants to do in your setting. But you won't discover that without diligent prayer.

My hope is that you will refuse to take the easy route. You need to care about His Church enough to fast and pray. You must believe you play a necessary role in the Church. Seek wisdom and direction from God. He has given you His Spirit so you can know and follow His will. There is no substitute for undistracted prayer. Our country needs to encounter churches that cannot be explained by strategic planning. And I believe everything inside you wants the Holy Spirit to move through you and do more than you can currently imagine. Start praying for this now.

FINAL THOUGHTS

You are going to see God soon. There's no way I can exaggerate how overwhelmed you will be. The most tragic mistake you can make on this earth is to underestimate how vulnerable you will feel when you see His face. And the wisest decisions you will make in life will be the ones you make with that final moment in mind.

All my life, I have battled a desire to be respected by others. Because of this, there have been many times I cowered out of a fear of rejection. I took my eyes off the future and did what was easiest in the moment. I deeply regret these moments.

The Bible tells countless stories of godly men and women who stood for what was right, even when it meant suffering pain and rejection. I often pray for God's grace, that He would bless me with the courage to follow their examples. I have prayed this for you as well. I really have.

> *"For, 'Yet a little while, and the coming one will come and will not delay; but my righteous one shall live by faith, and if he shrinks back, my soul has no pleasure in him.' But we are not of those who shrink back and are destroyed, but of those who have faith and preserve their souls."*
>
> Hebrews 10:37–39

Jesus is coming. I meet very few people in America who live as if they believe this. He gave the strongest warning ever written. It's called the book of Revelation. No one has ever given a stronger warning because no one else is capable of carrying out the threats He promised. Out of His love, He gave terrifying warnings to the Church of His day. Over and over, His message was repent or else. He then spent the rest of the book explaining what His "or else" looks like. He did this so no one will ignore His commands, yet we still do. Somehow we have become immune to warnings from almighty God.

What scares me most about His letters to the churches is the fact that some of those churches sound healthier than many I have visited in America, yet He gave them terrifying warnings. I wonder what He would say to us, considering what He said to them:

"Repent or else ..."

"I will come to you and remove your lampstand from its place" (Rev. 2:5).

"I will come to you soon and war against them with the sword of my mouth" (v. 16).

"I will throw [them] into great tribulation, unless they repent of her works, and I will strike her children dead. And all the churches will know that I am he who searches mind and heart, and I will give to each of you according to your works" (vv. 22–23).

"I will come like a thief, and you will not know at what hour I will come against you" (3:3).

"I will spit you out of my mouth" (v. 16).

These churches Jesus addressed would blend right in with the churches you find in your city. Some of them would even be lifted up as examples of church growth. This is why you can't afford to blindly follow or copy those who are "successful." You must come under the leadership of truly godly leaders or become one yourself.

Don't blindly follow the things I have written either. Study the Scriptures. Get alone with the Bible and the Holy Spirit. Seek Him with all your heart and surrender everything to Him. There cannot be anything you hold with a clenched fist, not even family. He is worth it.

Serve His Bride. Jesus is returning soon. We can't afford to be doing our own thing while His Bride lies unhealthy. We all want to be found at her bedside, broken over her condition, willing to sacrifice anything for her well-being.

> *Father, thank You for choosing us to be part of something so sacred. Forgive us for the times when our laziness weakened the Church or our pride divided her. Give us childlike faith to have an impact on the Church with Holy Spirit power.*
>
> *May Your Bride become attractive, devoted, and powerful beyond earthly explanation.*
>
> *May we each become consumed with her, all for Your glory. Keep our minds fixed on the battle, courageous and humble. Stir our affections daily so we can be found serving Your Bride faithfully when You return to judge. Amen.*

SURVIVING ARROGANCE

I wrestled the whole time I was writing this book because I knew that in the wrong hands, this book would hurt the Church rather than help. It's hard to speak directly about problems in the church because there are people who gravitate toward anything critical. Rather than using this book for self-evaluation, they will use it as ammunition against others. Pride runs rampant in the church, and knowledge has a way of increasing it (1 Cor. 8:1). Even now, I can picture arrogant people marching into their pastors' offices and confronting them with all of the shortcomings of their church. "Read this book by Francis Chan! He agrees with me that our church needs to change!" This attitude is the *last thing* the Church needs.

Many of you are filled with great excitement and passion to see reform. Your desire is to see the Church flourish. You want God to use you to bring change. But for some of you, He won't. You will fail miserably for one reason: you're not humble. He promises to oppose your efforts (James 4:6). Rather than being used by God to bring life to the Church, the Enemy will use you to destroy.

"God opposes the proud but gives grace to the humble."

James 4:6

With the last few pages of this book, I felt a need to address the arrogant in hopes of sparing the Church of further division. As I started to write, however, I realized that this rarely works. Have you ever tried to convince a proud person of his or her pride? Some of you reading this are extremely proud, but you can't see it because you're extremely proud. You read this paragraph and nod your head as though I am speaking about someone else. It felt a bit hopeless, so I decided to switch gears. Rather than trying to convict the proud, I decided to write some words to encourage those who have to live with the proud. I guess you can call it a leader's guide to loving the arrogant.

There have been times when I have gotten so angry or discouraged by critics. Neither is good for the Church. It feels like I meet pastors every week who are ready to quit under the barrage of criticism. The Church can't afford to lose any more servants. If you have ever felt this way, I'm writing to encourage you to not only persevere but thrive as you minister to the proud. Some of you have stopped leading, and I hope to convince you to come back. Some of you have run from your calling because you don't want to face the attacks. It's much easier to hide in your basement and start a blog or podcast in order to criticize others, but I want to challenge you to build. It's a lot easier to tear down a building than it is to build one. It's grueling, but the Church is worth it. The Church does not have enough leaders who are willing to be on the receiving end of criticism and blame. If we can humble ourselves and learn to absorb rants graciously, our best days can be ahead of us.

God wants the Church to be the one institution that loves authority. He wants us to be different, a strange group of people who actually love having a King and are grateful for His commands. His desire is for us to view church leaders as God's gifts to the Church since He sees them that way.

And he gave the apostles, the prophets, the evangelists,
the shepherds and teachers, to equip the saints for the
work of ministry, for building up the body of Christ.
Ephesians 4:11–12

God "gave" these leaders to the Church in order to bring her to maturity. When's the last time you heard someone refer to leaders as gifts?

Recently, I heard someone in the church say, "I love being under the leadership of the elders." That was so weird to hear! Someone is grateful for authority? I loved hearing it, but it was weird. Uplifting speech toward authority is rarely heard in our world, but this gives us the opportunity to stand out.

After all, we follow a King who is unlike any other in history. He is a King who gladly submitted to His Father. In fact, Jesus claimed He would only say and do what the Father told Him to say and do.

"So Jesus said to them, 'Truly, truly, I say to you,
the Son can do nothing of his own accord, but
only what he sees the Father doing. For whatever
the Father does, that the Son does likewise.'"

John 5:19

"For I have not spoken on my own authority, but
the Father who sent me has himself given me a
commandment—what to say and what to speak. And
I know that his commandment is eternal life. What
I say, therefore, I say as the Father has told me."

John 12:49–50

This kind of submission is often viewed as weak and degrading in our culture, yet this is the example of almighty Jesus. He submitted to leadership. Jesus had nothing but praise for His Father. This is unusual, but this is our example. He was a humble leader *and* a humble follower. There was nothing weak about His humility. The Church would become so attractive if His humility could be seen in all of us.

As I share these following principles, in no way am I saying I have mastered any of them. I am still prone to become angry, defensive, or frustrated, but these are the biblical principles that restore my mind. They have led to some growth in my character, and I hope they prove useful in your life as well. There is a way to minister to negative people in humility and grace. This won't ensure growth in their lives, but it will in your life.

COUNT IT ALL JOY

> *"Count it all joy, my brothers, when you meet trials of various kinds, for you know that the testing of your faith produces steadfastness. And let steadfastness have its full effect, that you may be perfect and complete, lacking in nothing."*

> James 1:2–4

You can't fully mature without being attacked. I know it doesn't feel right when the attacks come from within the Church. Nonetheless, God uses these situations to sanctify us. We all need a Judas in order to become like Jesus. When everyone around you loves you, it's nearly impossible to develop the character God wants for His children. Reasonable people do not aid your growth in the same way arrogant people do. We don't display Christian love when we love those who love us. It is when we love those who slander us that we demonstrate the love of Christ (Matt. 5:44–45). Find joy in sanctification. Challenge yourself to grow to the point where you become thankful for difficult people.

HUMBLY LISTEN

Just because something is said with the wrong attitude doesn't mean it's wrong information. A mistake I have made too often is to respond to pride with pride. There have been too many times when my goal was to bite my tongue and remain calm. Listening to find truth in their statements required another level of humility I didn't have.

I'm always amused and impressed when I read this story about David:

> *Then Abishai the son of Zeruiah said to the king, "Why should this dead dog curse my lord the king?*

Let me go over and take off his head." But the king
said, "What have I to do with you, you sons of
Zeruiah? If he is cursing because the LORD has said
to him, 'Curse David,' who then shall say, 'Why
have you done so?'" And David said to Ahishai and
to all his servants, "Behold, my own son seeks my
life; how much more now may this Benjaminite!
Leave him alone, and let him curse, for the LORD
has told him to. It may be that the LORD will look
on the wrong done to me, and that the LORD will
repay me with good for his cursing today." So David
and his men went on the road, while Shimei went
along on the hillside opposite him and cursed as
he went and threw stones at him and flung dust.

2 Samuel 16:9–13

Picture King David marching with his army. A fool comes along, throwing rocks at him and cursing him. When David's soldier asks if he can chop off the guy's head, David says to leave him alone. His reasoning? David was open to the possibility this man was sent from God! So he patiently endured the cursing, just in case it really was a message from God.

To be honest, I am rarely able to listen to proud people. I typically get defensive, combative, or sarcastic. However, there have been a few times recently, when by the grace of

God, I have been able to listen for truth while being disrespected. There have even been a couple times when I have thanked an unreasonable critic for showing me my sin. It's amazing how quickly humility can diffuse a tense situation. This is not to say that we should condone angry criticism. But as leaders, we need to set an example of humility and avoid the trap of becoming hypocritical. That will only add fuel to their fire.

FORGIVE THEM, THEY KNOW NOT WHAT THEY DO

In Romans 11, God warned the Gentiles not to get proud because they understood God in a way many Jews did not. Paul reminded them that it was by the grace of God their eyes were opened. Meanwhile, he said regarding some of the Jews, "God gave them a spirit of stupor, eyes that would not see and ears that would not hear, down to this very day" (v. 8). Paul's point was that any spiritual awareness was gifted from God, so it made no sense to boast.

Think of it this way: if I bought my son a new Ferrari (which would never happen), and he judged his friends who rode their bikes to school, it would be absurd. He should have the wisdom to see that he was a spoiled kid who did nothing to earn his car. It was handed to him. He has nothing to brag about. In the same way, if you have even an ounce of humility, it is only by of the grace of God. He blessed you with it. If we truly believe this, then it makes no sense to be angry at others for not having received the same grace. Thank God for any insight, wisdom, or humility He has graced you with. Quickly forgive anyone who has hurt you and pray God, by His mercy, would open their eyes.

PARTY WITH PROUD PEOPLE

"We who are strong have an obligation to bear with the failings of the weak, and not to please ourselves. Let each of us please his neighbor for his good, to build him up. For Christ did not please himself, but as it is written, 'The reproaches of those who reproached you fell on me.'"

Romans 15:1–3

I spent many years writing people off. In my immaturity, I didn't know how to love people who annoyed me. It was so much easier to just avoid them. I found ways to justify my actions, but ultimately it was displeasing to God. He commands us to "bear with the failings of the weak" (v. 1). He calls this our obligation. All of us tend to avoid arrogant people because they annoy *us*. God's response is that we can't make this about *us*. He tells us "not to please ourselves" (v. 1). It may be true that people have hurt our feelings, but we must learn to value God's Church more than our feelings. We can cause real damage to our churches when we want our feelings validated more than we want His Bride elevated.

I'm sure you can think of people in your life you wish would just disappear. Maybe there have even been times when you have prayed for God to remove certain individuals from the church. Proud people can be hard to live with, but avoiding them is not an option. We have an obligation to love and to suffer "reproach" as Christ did for us.

> *"Therefore the LORD waits to be gracious to you, and therefore he exalts himself to show mercy to you."*
>
> Isaiah 30:18

Despite every time the Israelites failed and rebelled and essentially spit on God's kindness toward them, He loved them enough to *wait* to be gracious to them. Unlike us, God is a perfectly holy King who never makes mistakes. How much more should we humans be willing to endure and show compassion for other people's weaknesses?

DON'T TOLERATE DIVISIVENESS

We are called to love proud people, but there is a time to put your foot down. Once they start to gossip, or speak negatively of leadership or church members, the rules change.

"As for a person who stirs up division, after
warning him once and then twice, have nothing
more to do with him, knowing that such a person
is warped and sinful; he is self-condemned."

Titus 3:10–11

Rarely do I see churches take this command seriously. The Church would be much healthier if we did. Proud people are prone to gossip, and that's when they have crossed the line that was drawn by God. It's crazy how quickly a divisive person can split a church. Many churches have been destroyed because leaders were unwilling to confront and remove divisive people. Scripture clearly states that after a couple of warnings, we should "have nothing more to do with him" (v. 10). It's not that we are condemning him. The passage states that "he is self-condemned," meaning he has done this to himself. If we refuse to remove these people, we become guilty of disobeying Scripture.

Most people believe it is unloving to ever remove someone from the church. In the name of compassion, they refuse to ever obey Scripture (Matt. 18:15–20, 1 Cor. 5; Titus 3:10–11). Please don't be fooled. This is not compassion; it is rebellion. We are not treating God's Church as sacred when we allow certain people to stay. We are permitting a human being to divide God's Holy Church while we do nothing about it. God hates this.

Earlier in the book I wrote about how David honored Saul because of his position, but have you ever noticed the actions of David's son, Absalom? Read 2 Samuel 15 some time. Absalom's spirit and actions are so prevalent in the Church today.

> *"And Absalom used to rise early and stand beside the way of the gate. And when any man had a dispute to come before the king for judgment, Absalom would call to him and say, 'From what city are you?' And when he said, 'Your servant is of such and such a tribe in Israel,' Absalom would say to him, 'See, your claims are good and right, but there is no man designated by the king to hear you.' Then Absalom would say, 'Oh that I were judge in the land! Then every man with a dispute or cause might come to me, and I would give him justice.' And whenever a man came near to pay homage to him, he would put out his hand and take hold of him and kiss him. Thus Absalom did to all of Israel who came to the king for judgment. So Absalom stole the hearts of the men of Israel.*

2 Samuel 15:2–6

Do you notice what Absalom said? He spoke negatively about David's leadership, but he did it in such a clever and careful way. He calmly spoke of how he wished things were different, and how he would do things differently if he was in charge. In so doing, he "stole the hearts of the men of Israel" (v. 6). There are Absaloms in every church, seeking to gain a following through clever speech. They convince you to question the existing leadership and talk about how they would do things differently. Like Absalom, it's spoken in a caring tone to mask the evil. Don't fall for it. There are already too many misguided people who boast of being a "safe place" because they are willing to listen to people's complaints and hurts without passing judgment on them. If you are one of those people, understand that this is not a gift; it's a weakness. It's people like you, who passively listen to gossip rather than confront it, that enable the Absaloms of the world to divide churches. You need to develop some courage. Don't allow anyone to divide God's Holy Church or slander His anointed leaders. If you hear anyone speak negatively about another believer, bring them directly to the person they are attacking. Be courageous enough to lead reconciliation. "Blessed are the peacemakers" (Matt. 5:9).

DON'T FALL FOR EVERY TEAR

Let me say that I am not trying to belittle those who have been hurt by a church or church leader. I wrote this book to point out areas where the Church is lacking. I'm not trying to brush off those who have faced abuse at the hands of others. I am asking you to be aware that there are people in the Church who have become incredibly proficient at making themselves the victim of every story. They are professional victims, and this is usually rooted in pride. They learn that tears almost always ensure victory. If at first you don't succeed, cry and cry again. Once you cry, you make yourself the victim which means the person who made you sad must be the bad guy. Sobbing can be a powerful weapon.

I still remember the first time I dealt with this. Twenty years ago, I was speaking at a singles' conference. After the message, a group of people lined up to talk. Some came for counsel; others came with encouragement. One girl was casually telling me about sin in her life. As I explained the seriousness of the sin and encouraged her repentance, she fell to the ground. She curled into a ball, started crying loudly, was shaking, and said, "You're scaring me! I don't feel safe!" Instant victory. Now she had everyone looking at me like I was the bad guy. It was now my duty to put my hand on her shoulder and apologize for hurting her. The attention was off her sin and onto her hurt. Suddenly, I was the sinner and she was the victim. Checkmate! Now I looked uncaring if I just stared at her rather than apologizing and coddling. Not only that, but she could then cry to others about how much I hurt her.

Obviously, many tears are genuine and warrant our comfort. We definitely don't want to grow calloused toward the hurts of others. Like parents, we must learn to distinguish between real cries, manipulative cries, and cries for attention. The compassionate side of you will be tempted to comfort everyone who weeps, but that isn't always the most loving thing to do for them. The apostle Paul didn't regret causing tears. In fact, he explained that grief can be a good thing. Out of love for the Corinthians, Paul grieved them in the hope of repentance.

> *"For even if I made you grieve with my letter, I do not regret it—though I did regret it, for I see that that letter grieved you, though only for a while. As it is, I rejoice, not because you were grieved, but because you were grieved into repenting. For you felt a godly grief, so that you suffered no loss through us. For godly grief produces a repentance that leads to salvation without regret, whereas worldly grief produces death."*
> 2 Corinthians 7:8–10

Let's love people enough to help them leave their own pity parties so they can spend their lives drawing attention to God rather than themselves.

DON'T DWELL

> *"Finally, brothers, whatever is true, whatever is honorable, whatever is just, whatever is pure,*

whatever is lovely, whatever is commendable,
if there is any excellence, if there is anything
worthy of praise, think about these things."

Philippians 4:8

One of the biggest mistakes we make is to allow proud people to consume our thoughts. We allow our minds to replay the instances when others have offended us. This robs us of our joy and robs God of the worship He deserves.

Ephesians 5 explains that the Spirit-filled person continually worships and gives thanks. Satan hates the sound of our praise and thanksgiving, so he makes it his mission to disrupt worship. He loves when our minds are filled with frustration and discouragement rather than praise. Don't give him the victory. Control your thoughts.

PRAISE JESUS

This has helped me tremendously. Whenever I feel like I'm being mistreated, I start worshipping Jesus. I tell Him I am amazed by what He pulled off. Any mistreatment I have faced is an absolute joke compared to the horrors Christ endured. How on earth does an almighty Creator allow His creation to torture Him? Even as I write this, I am marveling again at His humility. Instead of beating myself up for my lack of humility, I praise Jesus for His.

I have found that the more I stare at His humility, the more I praise Him and want to be like Him. Take some time now to praise Jesus, "the founder and perfecter of our faith, who for the joy that was set before him endured the cross, despising the shame, and is seated at the right hand of the throne of God" (Heb. 12:2).

WIN AT ALL COSTS

I'm too competitive. At times I get consumed with winning an argument. Love goes out the window, and I get obsessed with proving I'm right. I hate that about myself. When I am obsessed with winning, it means I am not obsessed with Jesus. So I have tried to change my thinking.

Maybe there's a way for those of us who have been dealt a hyper-competitive nature to use this to our advantage. After all, there is a verse that tells us to compete: "Outdo one another in showing honor" (Rom. 12:10). Our competitions just look different, and our greatest victory is when we win the favor of God. Obviously, I'm not talking about some kind of works salvation. I am saying there are many verses that speak about God blessing the humble. While humility is a gift, it does not just passively appear. He commands us to humble ourselves. While it's something we pray for, it's also something we strive for. There's a verse that encourages me in my pursuit of humility. It's one of my favorites:

> *"For thus says the One who is high and lifted up,*
> *who inhabits eternity, whose name is Holy: 'I dwell*
> *in the high and holy place, and also with him who*
> *is of a contrite and lowly spirit, to revive the spirit of*
> *the lowly, and to revive the heart of the contrite.'"*
>
> Isaiah 57:15

This is the end of the book, so you have time to read this verse over and over. I couldn't think of a better verse to end this section. Memorize it. Write it out. Paint it on your wall. Text it to your friends. Meditate on every word. If this doesn't motivate you to fight for humility, nothing will. Our Holy God offers to dwell with you if you have a lowly and contrite spirit.

NOTES

CHAPTER 2

1. Tim Sharp, "How Far Is Earth from the Sun?," Space.com, October 18, 2017, www.space.com/17081-how-far-is-earth-from-the-sun.html.

CHAPTER 3

1. "Religious Service Attendance (Over Time)," Association of Religion Data Archives, accessed May 23, 2018, www.thearda.com/quickstats /qs_105_t.asp.

2. Søren Kierkegaard, *Provocations: Spiritual Writings* (Walden, NY: Plough, 2002), 168.

3. Alan Hirsch, *The Forgotten Ways: Reactivating Apostolic Movements* (Grand Rapids, MI: Brazos, 2016), 34–35.

4. Mike Breen, *Building a Discipling Culture: How to Release a Missional Movement by Discipling People Like Jesus Did*, 3rd ed. (Greenville, SC: 3DM Publishing, 2017), n.p.

5. David Platt, *Radical Together: Unleashing the People of God for the Purpose of God* (Colorado Springs: Multnomah, 2011), 59–60.

CHAPTER 5

1. Mike Breen, *Building a Discipling Culture: How to Release a Missional Movement by Discipling People Like Jesus Did*, 3rd ed. (Greenville, SC: 3DM Publishing, 2011), 11.

2. A. W. Tozer, *Tozer for the Christian Leader: A 365-Day Devotional* (Chicago: Moody, 2001), September 2.

CHAPTER 6

1. Hugh Halter, *Flesh: Bringing the Incarnation Down to Earth* (Colorado Springs: David C Cook, 2014), 119.

CHAPTER 7

1. John Collins, "Anything Is Possible," Ironman, accessed May 24, 2018, www.ironman.com/#axzz5GSFlau30.

2. "Evangelical Growth," Operation World, accessed May 24, 2018, www.operationworld.org/hidden/evangelical-growth.

CHAPTER 8

1. *Madagascar*, directed by Eric Darnell and Tom McGrath (Glendale, CA: DreamWorks Animation, 2005).

2. Alan Hirsch, *The Forgotten Ways: Reactivating Apostolic Movements* (Grand Rapids, MI: Brazos, 2016), 176.

3. David Garrison, "Church Planting Movements: The Next Wave?," *International Journal of Frontier Missions* 21, no. 3 (Fall 2004): 120–21.

CHAPTER 9

1. Tim Chester and Steve Timmis, *Total Church: A Radical Reshaping around Gospel and Community* (Wheaton, IL: Crossway, 2008), 18.

2. *Read Scripture*, v.7.0.0 (Crazy Love Ministries, 2018), readscripture.org.

3. Reach Beyond, *Great Commission Action Guide*, accessed May 25, 2018, https://reachbeyond.org/Advocate/RBActionGuide.pdf.

4. "25 Best Global Companies to Work For," Fortune, accessed May 25, 2018, http://fortune.com/global-best-companies/hyatt-19/.

5. "How Many Employees Does Airbnb Have?," Quora, November 14, 2015, www.quora.com/How-many-employees-does-Airbnb-have-1.

6. Avery Hartmans, "Airbnb Now Has More Listings Worldwide Than the Top Five Hotel Brands Combined," Business Insider, August 10, 2017, www.businessinsider.com/airbnb-total-worldwide-listings-2017-8.

7. "New York City, New York Population 2018," World Population Review, accessed May 25, 2018, http://worldpopulationreview.com/us-cities/new-york-city-population/.

8. Lyle E. Schaller, *The Interventionist* (Nashville: Abingdon, 1997), 70.

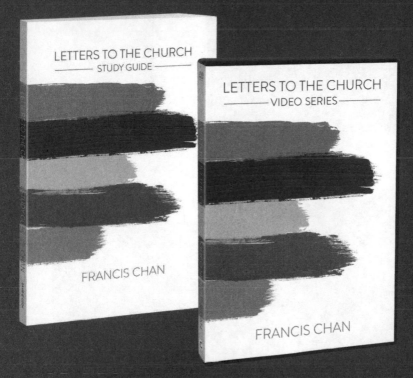

For your church.
For your small group.
For you.

Discover why so many others have been impacted by the
challenging message of Francis Chan.

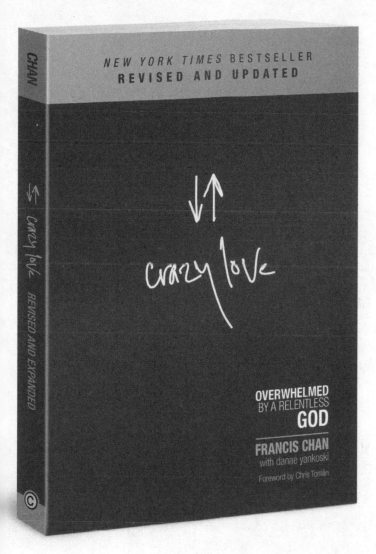